Frederic William Farrar

The silence and the voices of God, with other sermons

Frederic William Farrar

The silence and the voices of God, with other sermons

ISBN/EAN: 9783337085957

Printed in Europe, USA, Canada, Australia, Japan

Cover: Foto ©Lupo / pixelio.de

More available books at **www.hansebooks.com**

IN PRESS.

BY THE SAME AUTHOR:

THE LIFE OF CHRIST.

Two volumes, 8vo.

E. P. DUTTON AND COMPANY,

𝔓𝔲𝔟𝔩𝔦𝔰𝔥𝔢𝔯𝔰,

713 BROADWAY, NEW YORK.

AND THE

VOICES OF GOD,

WITH OTHER SERMONS.

BY

FREDERIC W. FARRAR, D.D., F.R.S.

Late Fellow of Trinity College, Cambridge; Master of Marlborough College,
and Chaplain in Ordinary to the Queen.

NEW YORK:
E. P. DUTTON & COMPANY,
713 BROADWAY,
1874.

THE MIDDLETON STEREOTYPE CO., GREENPORT, L. I.

TO

THE REV. CANON WESTCOTT, D.D.,

REGIUS PROFESSOR OF DIVINITY IN THE UNIVERSITY
OF CAMBRIDGE,

I DEDICATE THESE SERMONS

WITH CORDIAL GRATITUDE

AND

WITH SINCERE ADMIRATION AND ESTEEM.

PREFACE.

THE three first sermons, which give their title to this little volume, were preached before the University of Cambridge, and are published by the request of the Vice-Chancellor. I have added to them a few other sermons in deference to the wishes of those who heard them delivered, and desired to possess them in a permanent form.

CONTENTS.

I.

SILENCE AND VOICES.

1 SAM. iii. 10. Speak; for thy servant heareth............ PAGE. 11

II.

THE VOICE OF CONSCIENCE.

ROM. ii. 15. Their conscience also bearing witness......... 39

III.

THE VOICE OF HISTORY.

Ps. xlvi. 6. The heathen make much ado, and the kingdoms are moved; but God hath shewed His voice, and the earth shall melt away.................................... 60

IV.

WHAT GOD REQUIRES.

MICAH vi. 6–8. Wherewith shall I come before the Lord, and bow myself before the high God? shall I come before Him with burnt offerings, with calves of a year old? Will the Lord be pleased With thousands of rams, or with ten thousands of rivers of oil? shall I give my firstborn for my transgression, the fruit of my body for the sin of my soul? He hath shewed thee, O man, what is good; and what doth the Lord require of thee, but to do justly, and to love mercy, and to walk humbly with thy God?....... 93

V.

AVOIDANCE OF TEMPTATION.

MATTHEW iv. 5-7. Then the devil taketh Him up into the holy City, and setteth Him on a pinnacle of the temple, and saith unto Him, If Thou be the Son of God, cast Thyself down: for it is written, He shall give His angels charge concerning Thee: and in their hands they shall bear Thee up, lest at any time Thou dash Thy foot against a stone. Jesus said unto him, It is written again, Thou shalt not tempt the Lord thy God.................... 107

VI.

THE CONQUEST OVER TEMPTATION.

1 COR. x. 13. There hath no temptation taken you but such as is common to man: but God is faithful, who will not suffer you to be tempted above that ye are able; but will with the temptation also make a way to escape, that ye may be able to bear it................................ 125

VII.

WISDOM AND KNOWLEDGE.

PROVERBS iv. 7. Wisdom is the principal thing; therefore get wisdom: and with all thy getting get understanding. 147

VIII.

WORKING WITH OUR MIGHT.

PAGE.

2 CHRON. xxxi. 21. And in every work that he began in the service of the House of God, and in the Law, and in the Commandments, to seek his God, he did it with all his heart, and prospered 165

IX.

PHARISEES AND PUBLICANS.

LUKE xviii. 9. And he spake this parable unto certain that trusted in themselves that they were righteous, and despised others 183

X.

TOO LATE.

LUKE xix. 42. If thou hadst known, even thou, at least in this thy day, the things which belong unto thy peace! but now they are hid from thine eyes 207

XI.

PRAYER, THE ANTIDOTE TO SORROW.

LUKE xxii. 44. And being in an agony, He prayed......... 225

I.

SILENCE AND VOICES.

"Muto non è, come altri credi, il cielo
Sordi siam noi, a cui l' orecchio serra
Lo strepito insolente della terra."

Speak, for thy servant heareth.—1 SAM. iii. 10.*

MAN is a mystery to himself, and he is surrounded by mysteries unnumbered. In the ordinary practical business of life,—in the common task of everyday existence,—he finds indeed no difficulty; and for millions of his race, for millions who spend their days in servile toil, and whose horizon is spanned by the little circle of ordinary interests,—the 'Enigmas of Life' would be a meaningless expression. Absorbed in a sordid or a sensual present, they have never wondered whence they came, or whither they are going;—they neither question of the future, nor dream about the past. It was the daily self-examination of one of the most eminent of saints, *Bernarde, ad quid venisti?* "Bernard, for what purpose art thou here?" but

* Preached before the University of Cambridge, April 27, 1873.

there are whole races of mankind, to whom, shut in by the narrowing walls of natural dulness or involuntary ignorance, such questions have never taken shape. And yet these too, my brethren, are our brothers; these too are heirs of our common immortality: for these two the great sun shines in heaven, and the pure dew falls upon the sleeping fields; over these, no less than over ourselves, broods unseen, yet ever present, the atmosphere of Eternity; and it is as possible, we believe, for these, as for earth's most gifted and most glorious children, to stand redeemed before the Great White Throne. And why?—Because, under all diversities, the essential condition of mankind is one; because, whatever we may fancy, God is οὐ προσωπολήπτης — no respecter of persons;—because intelligence or dulness, knowledge or ignorance, rank or obscurity, wealth or indigence, these, and all other evanescent or artificial distinctions between man and man, are non-existent in the eyes of God, or rather are only existent as conditions which in no wise affect the innermost reality of his being;— which reality depends on this alone,—whether Man is seeing the face, and holding the hand, and listening to the voice of God, or whether that face has vanished from him, that hand been withdrawn, that voice has first sunk into silence, then faded from memory, then been banished from belief.

My brethren, in this matter let us not be deceived. We of this land, of this century, of this University are, by God's grace, heirs of the treasuries of the world. Nothing profound has been ever thought, nothing enchanting ever imagined, nothing noble ever uttered, nothing saintly or heroic ever done, which is not or may not be ours. For us Plato and Shakespeare thought; for us Dante and Milton sang; for us Bacon and Newton toiled; for us Angelo and Raphael painted; for us Benedict and Francis lived saintly lives; for the heritage of our liberty have myriads of heroes perished on the battle-field, and for the purity of our religion hundreds of martyrs sighed away their souls amid the flames. But let us not pride ourselves on this our glorious inheritance, or falsely dream that this alone will avail us anything, or that we are favorite children in the great family of God. Certainly since to us much has been given, from us much shall be required; but, nevertheless, the poorest and most squalid savage, the most oppressed and ignorant slave, shares with us a blessing and a mystery incomparably more transcendent than any of these,—as much more transcendent as the sun is vaster and brighter than the earth,—in that, to all of us alike God speaks; in that for all of us alike, Christ died. To these, no less than to us, it is possible so to live, in obedience to the law of God, that Life, even amid its sin and suffering, may still echo with the distant songs of a lost Paradise; and so to die, that death may be none other than the house of God, and the gate of heaven. The earthly gifts which make man pride himself above his fellow-man are all perishable; it is those things only which cannot be shaken that shall remain. "Know" (and, when we read such utterances, and contrast them with the moaning, groping, disbelieving, despairing faithlessness of an increasing mass of modern literature, we seem to be breathing the atmosphere of another and a better world!) "Know that all are equal before the Lord, and that men are born for holiness as the trees of the forrest for light." Yes, *holiness* is the one thing needful; whether there be prophecies, they shall fail; whether there be tongues, they shall cease; whether there be knowledge, it shall vanish away; earthly learning, and earthly endowments are but as the grass, and as the flower: "the grass withereth, the flower fadeth, because the Spirit of the Lord bloweth upon it: the grass withereth, the flower fadeth, but *the Word of our God shall stand for ever.*" *

The Word of our God—that, and that alone; and man, only as he listens to that Word, only as he is in harmony with that God. The earth may be shattered, and the heavens pass like a shrivelled scroll; but not the soul of man, which hath become partaker of God's Eternity. The one thing then of real and infinite importance to us, is, not the fruit of our studies, not the success of our efforts, not the things for which men toil and weary themselves and sigh, not anything whereby we are distinguished from other men, but this only, which affects us in common with *all* other men, whether our ears are quick to hear, and our hearts zealous to obey the voice of God. To do this is safety: not to do this is misery and failure: nay, to do this is life, and to do it not is to make life itself an initiation into death. And therefore, for these three Sundays on which it is my high privilege to address you, I would speak, feebly indeed and unworthily, but yet earnestly, on some fragment of

* Is. xl. 7, 8.

this great subject—*The Silence and the Voices of God.*

And surely the subject is not a needless one. It may be a sad and startling fact, but it *is* a fact, that, more and more among us, more and more after eighteen Christian centuries, more and more, though History has been full of lightnings and thunderings and voices, yea, though the Word of God has been made flesh and tabernacled among us, there are men, men alas! of learning and genius, who not only refuse to listen to God's voice, but even deny that God has ever spoken, deny even that He is. Yes, in the dismal advance of atheism, not content to repudiate the Lord that bought, and the Spirit that striveth with them, men are beginning openly to debate, in the blindness of their self-sufficiency, whether there be so much as a God who created them. And when we meet with such, what shall we say? My brethren, the proof of God's existence wholly transcends the region of argument, nor is it any proposition which can be coldly reasoned out by the finite understanding. If indeed a man of base motives and guilty deeds, a blasphemer, a murderer, an adulterer, one whose life is an organized battle against the will and law of God, if such a man denies God, of what use is it to say to him with the fervid Father, *Et tu tamen eum nosti, dum odtisi?** Nay rather, must we not say to him that he is too deeply pledged and enlisted against the truth to be convinced of it? that as he has chosen to live having no hope, and without God in the world? so for him there *is* no God in the world? He hath said it in his heart, and who, in such a matter, shall neutralize the deadly bias of his will? what more can we say to him, and what better can we hope for him, than that, if the weak words of man fail to pierce the hardened intellect, God's own power may, through strange Providences, correct and convert His erring child and lead him by the hand into the Temple of a pure Faith through the open portals of a holier and nobler life? But when a man of whom we know no evil, when a man of whose life Charity is sure that it is honorable and innocent, when such a man says with Diagoras, that there is no God, or with Protagoras that he cannot tell whether there be or not,† then if the invisible things

---

* Tert. *de testim. Animae*, iii.
† ἴσασι γὰρ οὐχ ἑκόντες καὶ λέγουσιν ἄκοντες . . . κἂν μὴ εἶναι φῇς ὡς Διαγόρας κἂν ἀγνοεῖν τι φῇς ὡς Πρωταγόρας. Max. Tyr. *Dissert.* xvii. ep. 5. Cic. *de Nat. Deorum*. I. i. Diog. Laert. ix. 51. Arist. *Nub.* 830, etc.

of Him from the creation of the world be not clearly seen, being understood by the things that are made, even His eternal power and Godhead,—if God's works be disregarded, is it likely that Man's logic will avail? Can we construct a syllogism, more overpowering for his conviction than " the starry heavens above ? " can we write a book of evidences more potent to his conscience than "the moral law within?" A society for the defence of Christianity may have its own to do, but will it persuade the unbeliever, if the voices of the sea and the mountains fail ? A man may stand, if he will, amid the mirth and music of a breathing summer day, when all the air is vocal with whispering trees, and singing birds, and the quivering of insects wings, and assert to us, contemptuously, that all is silent : what can we answer him save that it *is* silent to the dull deaf ear ? A man may close his eyes if he will till they are blind, and then, standing in the burning noonday, may defy us to prove that there is a sun in heaven : what need we care to say to him in answer, but that we see its splendor, but that we feel its warmth ? What *can* we say to such, but that which even a heathen said, " God is within thee, and is thy God ; thou carriest God about with thee and knowest

Him not."* And may we not say, my brethren, that as for ourselves we know God; we hear His voice; we see His face; His name is on our foreheads? In joy He increases and purifies our joy; in sorrow He heals and sanctifies our sorrows; in sin He punishes and forgives our sins. And you, self-honoring children of a cold and faithless generation, if such be here, you, who have invested so much of modern thought with the clammy and creeping mist of our uncertainties and your negations, if ye cannot yourselves believe in God, be content at least in your own sad non-belief; and, however much ye may be puffed up by the pride of an imaginary emancipation, try not, in your cruel kindness, in your condescending pity, try not to rob us of Him. Try not to induce us to exchange for your mean and flickering tapers our "offspring of heaven first-born;" or to enlighten our darkness by putting out our sun. Or try your very utmost, but it will be in vain. We too are biassed. We desire not this strong delusion sent us that we should believe a lie. For to lose God is not, as you say,

* ὁ θεὸς ἔνδον ἐστὶ καὶ ὁ ὑμέτερος δαίμων ἐστί θεὸν περιφέρεις τάλας καὶ ἀγνοεῖς. Epict. *Dissert.* i. 14, 16.

to be robbed of some "*mentis gratissimus error;*" it is to lose our life. But we *cannot* lose it. Where you argue, we feel. Where you doubt, we know, Where you hesitate, we are certain. Where you deny, we live. Hold yourselves, if ye will and must, to be the sport and prey of every angry circumstance and every pitiless law, but we will trust in the name of the Lord our God. In the cold, in the storm, in the darkness, prefer if ye will to wander and stumble, without a comforter and without a friend, but we will grope for our Father's hand. And never have we, never hath any man groped for that hand in vain. "*Sanabiles fecit nationes terrae.*" Man may have gone astray, but not hopelessly; he may have been smitten with a leprosy, but it is not incurable. Oh, be it a little misfortune or a mighty agony, be it a childish trouble or a boyish folly, be it a transient disappointment of a lifelong difficulty, be it a sudden dereliction or a besetting sin, ye who have been sad, ye who have been weary, ye who have been sick with discontent or self-disgust, I challenge you to say whether you have ever sought Him and found his promise fail? whether you have ever sought Him without His holding forth to you in the very bitterness of death a green leaf from that Tree of Life that grows for the healing of the nations in the Paradise of God?

So then although, more and more, the icy wind of atheism, stealing through our literature with almost inarticulate whisper, is chilling the hearts of many, yet to counteract it, except by noble examples, except by Christian lives, appears to be but a futile labor. But there are myriads more, who, though they do not doubt the existence of God, yet deny His Providence. An image is before them, but there is SILENCE. For them He is inanimate as an idol. Clouds indeed and darkness are round about Him, but righteousness and judgment are not the habitation of His seat. The voices of man,—voices of blasphemy, voices of anguish, voices of adoration,—may break the eternal stillness, but they reach Him not, nor careth He, nor speaketh. How should He care? How should He speak? Hath he not abdicated in favor of His own works? What mean ye by your God, they say to us. What is He but the Universe? What is He but a vast formless Fate? What but a dread magnificence of Nature? What, but a fearful Uniformity of Laws? What, to take the latest of these philosophic utterances, what but "a stream of tendency flowing through the ages?"

And this, my brethren, if it be not unbelief, is just as hopeless and just as comfortless. We cannot trust in a blind destiny. We cannot love an awful uniformity of laws. "A stream of tendency flowing through the ages" may be a very philosophical conception of the God adopted by the insight or the criticism of the nineteenth century, but, unlike "our Father which is in heaven," it has "no ear for prayer, no heart for sympathy, no arm to save." This God is not our God, nor can *it* be our guide for ever and ever. And what follows? If God be not, or be as though He were not, then man is not or is as though he were not. For what then is man? What but a phantom, a vapor, a nothing,—the shadow of a dream moving amid dreams and shadows; at best one dying leaf in an illimitable forest; one unregarded rain drop in some immeasurable sea? And so, if life be but a semblance and death but an extinction, and if, amid an infinitude of Time peopled by myriads of existences, and an infinitude of Space teeming with innumerable worlds, man be an atom tossed out of nothingness, and destined to become but dust "blown about the desert or sealed within the iron hills;"—if this be so,—oh, dreary, dreary gospel of a darkness taking itself for exceptional enlightenment!—if God be nothing, and Man be nothing, what then is Virtue, and what is Truth? Virtue forsooth — though the Prophets and the Apostles and the Martyrs knew it not—is prudence; it is expedience; it is utility; it is enlightened self-interest; it is, to use their favorite formula, the "greatest happiness of the greatest number." And Truth is a subjective impression ultimately resolvable into particular conditions of the brain. My brethren, who can be moved by these dim abstractions, by these coarse materialisms? Who is the Lord—if this be He—who is the Lord that I should obey his voice? All is vanity, delusion, emptiness. All meaning is wiped out of life, as when a man wipeth a dish, wiping and turning it upside down; "*ut solum certum sit nihil esse certi nec miserius quicquam homine nec superbius.*" * If we sin, what does it matter to blind infinite Forces which may crush us, but cannot love? If we repent, what will the Æons and the Spaces care for our repentance? Are we any better than what the Greek atheist said we were, "dumb animals, driven through the mid-

* Pliny.

night upon a rudderless vessel, over a stormy sea?" "Let us eat and drink, for to-morrow we die." Yes, then that bitter description is true,—"Seated between the tomb of his fathers whom he has disowned, and the cradle of his children for whom he feels only a bitter pity, man is no more than a miserable puppet, condemned to play I know not what lugubrious comedy before I know not what icy spectators." *

And though these opinions, and such as these, have for the young all the "fascination of corruption,"—though they have all that destroying and agonizing beauty which the great painter infused into the horror of the Gorgon's countenance, on which men must gaze though it turned them into stone,†—yet God forbid that there should be many of you, my younger hearers, who should have subtly slidden into such treacherous unbeliefs. Yet they spring alas! from sources far beneath the soil; and many who have never said "There is no God," have yet found a self-deceiving excuse for sin in "Tush, God careth not for it, He hideth away his face, and shall never see it." And alas! the very best among us all fails too often to realize, as a guiding thought

* Montalembert. † The Medusa of Leonardo da Vinci.

in life, that God *does* speak, and speaks *to us*, and speaks distinct messages in voices awfully articulate; or, even when we believe it with all our hearts, how little are we rea!y always, in the midnight as in the noonday, to say, with bowed head and folded hands, "Speak Lord, for thy servant heareth." The Jews, in a legend that is not meaningless, tell us how, on the Mount, the great law-giver needed no human sustenance, because the subtle harmonies of the universe so filled his soul as to satisfy and sustain his whole being with their heavenly diapason; but when he came down out of the rolling clouds, the vesture of decay closed his ears and he heard no longer, and hungered for earthly food. Is it not so with us? Times there are when we hear the voice of God walking in the garden in the cool of the day, yea, when we hear it all the day long; and there are other times when we too listen with fainting hearts to those who tell us that we have but mistaken the pulse of our own beings for a sound above us; and that the universe wherein we live has long been smitten with the curse of silence. Oh, they do not lack for arguments! Around every step of our career on earth the mystery of the Infinite rises like a wall of adamant, and the limitation of our faculties falls like a curtain of darkness. Look, they say, at all this pain and misery and evil; how is it reconcilable with the Being of a God at once omnipotent and all-loving? Look at the myriads of mankind who have lived only as the beasts live, and died as the fool dieth. Look at all the evidences of "insane religion, degraded art, merciless war, sullen toil, detestable pleasure and vain hope or vile, in which the nations of the world have lived; so that it seems as if the race itself were still half-serpent, not yet extricated from the clay, a lacertine brood of bitterness, the track of it on the leaf a glittering slime, and in the sand a useless furrow;"* or in language less full of scorn, "see," they say, "how generation after generation of the young rush sanguine into the arena, generation after generation of the old step weary into the grave; how the beautiful and the noble are cut off in youth, while the stained and mean drag their ignominy through a long career. Look at the chastisements that do not chasten; the trials that do not purify; the sorrows that do not elevate; the pains and privations that harden the tender heart, but do not soften the stubborn will; the virtues that dig their own grave; the light that

* Ruskin.

leads astray."* Or need we look, they ask, beyond
our own little lives? how often is the folly of a moment the anguish of a life! In one instant a deed
is done, a choice is made,

> And there cometh a mist, and a weeping rain,
> And life is never the same again:

yet no voice from heaven speaks, no angel flashes
from the blue. And if the light does not shine, why
at least does not the thunder roll? men do wrong and
prosper; men do right and die in defeat and darkness. On the fields which the usurer has wrung
from the orphan, the sun shines and the harvest
waves; and no midnight dreams haunt the pillow
of the seducer, as he lies down to sleep as softly as
the innocent and the just. "Blaspheme God as
you will; deny God, if you wish to do so," says one
in a recent work of fiction; "do all the evil that you
possibly can do, and this sweet moonlight which
seems to rise out of the waves, will shine no less
sweetly for you than for me, and will conduct us
both to our quiet homes."†

My brethren, I shall not attempt to answer all
these objections from the supposed silences of God.

---
* *Enigmas of Life*, W. R. Grey, p. 210.
† Alphonse Karr, *Le Chemin le plus court*, p. 70.

God makes no ado: He does not defend himself: He suffers men to blaspheme; His enemies make a murmuring but He refrains. And as for these, many of them are false generalizations, many are distorted facts, some are acknowledged mysteries, some are wilful perversions of the truth: most of them may be reduced to this—that God's ways are in the sea, and His paths in the great waters, and His footsteps are not known. But further, much of this, yea, and more than all this, may alas! to those who utter it be awfully true. To men, to nations, sometimes almost to a whole world, God *is* silent: there *is* no God. Their eyes are blinded, so that they cannot see; their ears closed that they cannot hear. Aye, but it is a penal silence, a retributive blindness. They who love the darkness, have it. To those who will not listen, God does not speak: καθὼς οὐκ ἐδοκίμασαν τὸν Θεὸν ἔχειν ἐν ἐπιγνώσει παρέδωκεν αὐτοὺς ὁ Θεὸς εἰς ἀδόκιμον νοῦν.* Like avenges like: there is a terrible resemblance between the retribution and the crime: the choice that *will not* discern is punished in kind, punished even here by the mind that *cannot*. And then the whole universe becomes a gulf of silence, a void of blackness.

* Rom. i. 28.

They suffer, and there is no God; they sin, and there is no Redeemer; they despair, and there is no Comforter. The Jews, who with all their deadly perversity yet had many a flash of moral insight, knew this truth too well. God had spoken to them, they said, first, face to face as to Adam in Paradise; then only by the Urim; then only by dreams; then only by prophets; then only by the vague uncertainties of the daughter of a voice, which was but to the few an intelligible utterance, to the many but an articulate rolling of the distant thunder-peal. And as His voices sounded fainter and fainter, so did He withdraw farther and farther, as the sins of men assumed a deeper and deeper dye, until now He is but in the seventh and inmost heaven infinitely far, and seemed awhile to have left them to their fate. Yes, it is even so in the individual heart of man. God forgotten is God ignored; God ignored is God doubted of; God doubted of is God denied; God denied, sooner or later is God detested.

Aye, but on the other hand, to seek God is to find; and to listen is to hear; and to hear is to know and love; so that, to His saints, day unto day uttereth speech and night unto night sheweth knowledge, and "God is a declaratory God, speaking in ten thousand voices, and the whole year is one Epiphany, one day of manifestation."

1. He speaks to us, for instance, in Nature; and even while I say it, I can imagine at once how impatiently the cynic will sneer at what he will regard as a poetic fancy which has been worn threadbare into a deceptive platitude. It was so in the days of the Preacher, "He hath made everything beautiful in his time: also He hath set the world in their hearts so that no man can find out the work that God maketh." And so they cannot even learn that one lesson which to us comes intuitively and at once, that Nature is but visible spirit: that God *is*, and that He is a God of Love. Not to the base, not to the sensual, not to the cold cynic, not to the insolent scorner, but

> " Every bird that sings,
> And every flower that stars the elastic sod,
> And every breath the radiant summer brings,
> *To the pure spirit* is a Word of God."

And that you may rather listen I will not state it in my own words, but will quote here the language of one who is dubious about many Christian truths, and I will quote him to shew why it is that, standing with uncovered head and awful reverence in the mighty Temple of the Universe, a believer holds that God loves him, and wills his happiness. "The earth," he says, "is sown with pleasures, as the heaven is studded with stars; and when a man has not been happy in life, we do not hesitate to declare that he has missed one of the aims of his existence. The path of the years is paved and planted with enjoyments. Flowers the noblest and the loveliest,—colors the most gorgeous and the most delicate,—odors the sweetest and the subtlest, —harmonies the most soothing and the most stirring,—the sunny glories of the day,—the pale Elysian graces of the moonlight,—'silent pinnacles of aged snow' in one hemisphere,—the marvels of tropical luxuriance in another,— the serenity of sunsets, the sublimity of storms,— everything is bestowed in boundless profusion : we can conceive or desire nothing more exquisite or perfect than that which is around us every hour." That then is one revelation, but it is not all: for I add that Nature, which is but the visible translucence of a divine agency working upon material things, reveals to us also that this happiness is attainable only in the path of obedience,—that this "not-ourselves" (if any feel happier by the use of such pantheistic abstractions) is a not-ourselves which makes for righteousness. Winds blow this lesson to us, and waters roll it, and every leaf is inscribed with it, as those on which the Sybil wrote out her prophecies of old. "I dare to say it," writes a living author, "that because through all my life I have desired good, and not evil; because I have been kind to many, have wished to be kind to all, have wilfully injured none, therefore the morning light is yet visible to me on yonder hills:" and, "This we may discern assuredly; this every true light of science, every mercifully granted power, every wisely restricted thought, teach us more clearly day by day, that, in the heavens above and in the earth beneath, there is one continual and omnipotent presence of help and peace, for all men who know that they live, and remember that they die."

And oh, if any of you, even now, in your early days, have lost this lofty faith,—if, amid the glories of the world on which your lot is cast, you feel no "presence which disturbs you with the sense of elevated thoughts," or at least will not acknowledge that that presence is the presence of our God—boast not of this as though it were a sign of your unbiassed genius, or your intellectual superiority, but rather blush for it, if it be, as it often is, the Nemesis of a faithless disobedience,—or, if it be not, if it have come to you in a holy, and a humble, and a self-denying life, at the best weep for it as the worst curse which could have smitten your life with an irreparable blight; weep for it, if God give you the grace of tears, and pray, aye, even pray to the merciful Father in whom you have ceased to have a living faith, that He may save you from yourselves, and save the life which He has given you, with all its divine possibilities, and all its heavenly aspirations, from being dwarfed and degraded into "a tale

> "Told by an idiot, full of sound and fury,
> Signifying *nothing*."

2. And this God who thus reveals Himself to us in Nature, reveals Himself also in the Moral Law. It needed no voice from the rolling darkness, it needed no articulate thunder leaping among the fiery hills, to persuade mankind that "God spake these words and said." For that law was written on their hearts, their conscience also bearing them witness. The Jews believe that the souls of all Jews, for generations yet unborn, were summoned from their antenatal home to hear the Deliverance of the Fiery Law; and, when a Jew is charged with

wrong by another, he says, "My soul too has been on Sinai." But it is not the souls of Jews only, but of all mankind who have been there. It is there that they learnt that αὐτοδίκαιον which is unchangeable but by the Will of God. Nay, not there, but long before the volcanic forces upheaved from the bases of the world those granite crags, whenever first the dead clay began to flush and breathe with the unconsuming fire, then and there were learnt these eternal distinctions of right and wrong :

οὐ γάρ τι νῦν γε κᾳχθές, ἀλλ' ἀεί ποτε
ζῇ ταῦτα, κοὐδεὶς οἶδεν ἐξ ὅτου 'φάνη*

"In highest heaven they had their birth, neither did the mortal race of men beget them, nor shall oblivion ever put them to sleep ; the power of God is mighty in them, and groweth not old."† The great philosopher of Germany might well doubt of all things, till he had found that their certitude rested on the indestructible basis of duty.‡ If all else were shattered under our feet, that would still remain. False miracles themselves could not rob us of it. As in that grand legend of the Talmud, the tree might at the words of the doubter be trans-

* Soph. *Ant.* 458. † Soph. *Oed. Tyr.* 866. seqq. ‡ Kant.

planted from its roots; the rivulet might flow backward to its source; the walls and pillars of the conclave might crack; yea, a voice from heaven itself might preach another Law, yet neither rushing trees, nor backward flowing waters, nor bending roofs, nor miracles, nor mysterious voices should prevail against our solid and indestructible conviction, and the Eternal Himself should approve our constancy and exclaim from the mid glory of His Throne, " My sons have triumphed."*

3. And, once more, God speaks to us in Scripture; which means that He speaks to us in that revelation of Himself which He has vouchsafed to the lives and hearts of other men. He hath sent us prophets, rising up early and sending. Oh, my brethren, He who hath lost his belief, as thousands by their own impatience and to their own sorrow have lost it, has been robbed of a very blessed heritage. It is true that the Holy Scriptures have been wounded in the house of their friends; it is true that priests and theologians, in their craving for infallible authorities, have thrown up the mere letter of them between the intellect and God, making them an opaque barrier between us and

* Baba Metzia, f. 59.

Him of whom they were meant to be the crystal mirror. It is true that men, who were their professed defenders, have deprived them of their glory and their Universality, reading them under the vail of bigoted misconception, or through the lurid smoke of sectarian hate, making the Gospel of Life and Love and Liberty little better than "the remembrancer of damnation, and the messenger of Hell." And yet there, in all its human tenderness, in all its divine wisdom, like the lamp unquenched by the vapors of the charnel-house, for all who will use it rightly, that Holy and Blessed Book is laid up on the inviolable altar of truth and honesty, the eternal protest against the very sins which are committed in its name. Read it not with slavish superstition, not with a blind and literal Fetish worship, but in loving humility, in intelligent faith; and you, as myriads of your fathers have done, will find it, if not the only, yet assuredly the best, comfort in sorrow, the best warning in danger, the best hope in death: when all else is bitter, it still shall be sweeter than honey and the honey-comb, and when all else is dross, it shall be as ten times refined gold.

4 For lastly, let us never forget that it is there

chiefly—in the history that it records, in the sacraments which it perpetuates,—that we hear most clearly of all the Voice of God speaking to us by the divine lips of the Son of Man. It was thus, my brethren, that God revealed Himself, and if we reject that revelation, can we hope for any other? Is not this the very lesson of the New Testament:— "God, who at sundry times and in divers manners spake in times past unto the fathers by the prophets, hath, in these last days, spoken unto us by His Son?" And in the light of that truth, when we look at the ever-widening skepticism of this generation, do not the words of Christ, as recorded by the beloved Apostle, acquire a fresh and terrible significance:—" Ye have neither heard His voice at any time, nor seen His shape; and ye have not His word abiding in you: for, whom He hath sent, Him ye believe not?" Oh! let us hear that voice of the Son of God, for if we hear it not, we may hear no other; and they who hear it live. And, when we pour out the impassioned prayer of Luther, "Oh, my God, punish far rather with pestilence, with all the terrible sicknesses on earth, with war, with anything rather than that Thou be silent to us," let us remember that such silence is never that God doth not speak, but that we will not hear ; that whether we hear or not, and the degree in which we hear, depends upon ourselves ; that he who is of God heareth the words of God, and that, if we hear them not, it is because we are not of God. " The secret of the Lord is with them that fear Him, and He shall shew them His covenant;" but "the face of the Lord is against them that do evil, to root out the remembrance of them from the earth."

II.

THE VOICE OF CONSCIENCE.

"Se non che conscienzia m' assicura,
La buona compagnia che l' uom francheggia
Sotto l' osbergo del sentirsi pura."
DANTE, *Inf.* XXVIII. 115.

Their conscience also bearing witness.—ROM. ii. 15.*

I SPOKE in my last Sermon, my brethren, of the Silence and the Voices of God; I endeavored to shew that He does indeed speak to us, and speak to us continually, but that we may lose all sense of His utterance, and be wholly uninfluenced by it, as he who lives by the roar of a cataract is often unconscious of its sound: and then I spoke of His voice in Nature, His voice in Scripture, His voice in the Moral Law—above all, the voice wherewith God speaks to us by the lips of the Son of Man. To-day I would speak of another of His voices, of one which illustrates most clearly the methods whereby He deals with us, of that voice which is at once the most personal, the most peremptory, the most penetrating of all,—the voice of Conscience.

* Preached before the University of Cambridge, May 4, 1873.

And here I would say on the threshold that it is no part of my present duty to enter into the battle-field of modern materialism. If any rejoice to fling aside the old and inspiring conviction—that Man, "so noble in reason, so infinite in faculty, in form and moving so express and admirable, in action so like an angel, in apprehension so like a god," originated because God made him out of the dust of the earth and breathed into his nostrils the breath of life—and to take in exchange for it the humiliating and wholly undemonstrable hypothesis that he came into being by some accident of development, I know not how, from some film of protoplasm, I know not where—still Man *is*, and the facts of his inner being remain unchanged. Such beliefs, if they can be called beliefs, have indeed spread with a rapidity out of all proportion to the cogency of the arguments by which they are supposed to have been established. The great thinker who originated the theory, and whose name it is impossible to mention without admiration and respect, has distinctly declared himself against an atheistic materialism; and it has been left for his violent and reckless followers to maintain, to the outrage of all sense and of all religion, that Man sprang from a single primordial

THE VOICE OF CONSCIENCE. 41

moneres which was self-generated and self-evolved, and that therefore the belief in a Creator is unscientific and exploded. Enough of such: but even in England it has been thought a necessary sequel of this belief in Evolution to argue that Man, thus developed, proceeded to develop a moral sense out of social instincts fortified by hereditary transmission, and it is probable that very many even of my younger hearers have read that celebrated book on the Descent of Man, which professes—to quote the author's own words—to "approach the conscience exclusively from the side of natural history."

Well, if any man be content so to think, let him so think, and be fully persuaded in his own mind. The day has not yet arrived when it must be necessary for a Christian minister to preface his simplest teaching by a fresh proof of those grand truths which for well-nigh two millenniums have been the common heritage of advanced humanity. But since it is common in these times to try and represent the clergy as wilfully shutting their eyes to all recent investigation, I only allude to these forms of scientific assertion and negation, to shew that what is called the silence of ignorance may sometimes be the silence of repudiation, sometimes even the reticence of scorn.

In point of fact, however, no such theories will affect my main object. It is enough for me that even the most advanced materialist admits that whether, "approached exclusively from the side of natural history," or not, there is such a thing as Conscience and that its voice is heard in the soul of man; and I shall appeal to-day to nothing abstruser than these admitted facts of common experience.

Nor, again, is it my purpose to enter on any of the subtler questions of Moral Philosophy, or to reargue the ten-times-argued question whether or no Morality mean anything more than a system founded on social utility. In the Christian Church at least of a Christian University, it may, I suppose, even in this 19th century of illumination, have some weight that the word "usefulness does not once occur in the New Testament," nor was " Measure all things by a nice calculation of advantages," the language of Sinai, nor did our Lord and Master Jesus Christ ever place self-interest, however enlightened, on the throne of conscience, when He taught us the will of His Father in Heaven. Nor will any of the ordinary definitions of conscience here serve me. To call it "reflex approbation, or disapprobation,"—to describe it as "an imitation within ourselves of the government without us,"—to define it as "man, present to himself in his ethical conduct, and the object of his own approval or disapproval,"—may admirably illustrate the truth that when the wisest of the ancients defined virtue to be "a following of Nature," they were well aware that Man is a being of a mixt world, related to two worlds, the heavenly and the earthly,* and that though there be within us higher and lower principles of action, our nature is in reality represented by the higher and spiritual, not by the lower or animal, so that strong passions mean nothing more than weak reason. But alas! how little do such considerations touch the heart! how fully may they be admitted by the intellect, while they are ignored by the life! how few of the philosophers who held them were unaware of their practical impotence; or, as they themselves so sadly and so frankly confessed, were enabled, by the intellectual strength of these convictions, to approach, even distantly, to the glorious ideal of a holy or a noble life. No, this pale

* Anastas. Sinait. *De hominis creatione* (quoted by Harless, *Christian Ethics*, p. 49).

moonlight of an utilitarian or rational morality is not sufficient to guide the stumbling footsteps of man up the flinty or uphillward road : no misty meteors of a calculating philosophy, no feeble glimmerings of a developed instinct, no imaginary light of a fictitious faculty, will guide him there : nothing will save him from the precipices and pitfalls there, but that spirit of man which is the Lamp of God within him ; nothing less than the full sunlight of religion, yea, the Sun of Righteousness risen on the dark soul with healing in His wings.

An eminent and good man who lived to do much courageous work in the world, which to this day is bearing good fruit on the Western Continent, tells us a reminiscence of his childhood which will exactly illustrate my point of view. "When I was a little boy," he says, "in my fourth year, one fine day in spring my father led me by the hand to a distant part of the farm, but soon sent me home alone. On the way I had to pass a little pond, then spreading its waters wide; a rhodora in full bloom, a rare flower which grew only in that locality, attracted my attention, and drew me to the spot. I saw a little tortoise sunning himself in the shallow water at the roots of the flaming shrub. I lifted the stick I had in my hand, to strike the harmless reptile; for though I had never killed any creature, yet I had seen other boys do so, and I felt a disposition to follow their wicked examples. But all at once something checked my little arm, and a voice within me said clear and loud 'It is wrong!' I held my uplifted stick in wonder at the new emotion, the consciousness of an involuntary but inward check upon my actions, till the tortoise and the rhodora both vanished from my sight. I hastened home, and told the tale to my mother, and asked what it was that told me 'it was wrong.' She wiped a tear from her eye, and taking me in her arms said, 'Some men call it conscience, but I prefer to call it the voice of God in the soul of man. If you listen and obey it, then it will speak clearer and clearer, and always guide you right; but if you turn a deaf ear or disobey, then it will fade out, little by little, and leave you in the dark and without a guide. Your life depends on heeding that little voice.' She went her way," he continues, "careful and troubled about many things, and doubtless pondered them in her motherly heart: while I went off to wonder and think it over in my poor childish way; but I am sure no event in my life has made so deep and lasting an impression on me." Wise mother! Happy son! It is from such mothers that heroes spring; it is thus that are trained the saints of God. When the greatest of modern philosophers* exclaims, "O Duty, O wondrous power, that workest neither by insinuation, flattery, or threat, but merely by holding up the naked law in the soul, extortest for thyself reverence if not always obedience,— thou before whom all appetites are dumb however secretly they rebel, whence is thine origin?"—to such a question the Christian at least will answer without a moment's hesitation, and with all his heart, "Thine origin is God." The power of the conscience is simply paralyzed apart from the belief in God. If it be not, as St. Bernard calls it the *candor lucis aeternae et speculum Dei majestatis,*—if it be not man's consciousness of his relation to a Higher Being, whose law conditions the tendencies of his will,—it is nothing. Apart from God that moral law loses its meaning. It may be true, that the Ten Commandments, written on our hearts, obeyed in our lives, are sufficient to drive from us every assault of evil, but then they must *be* commandments; they must

* Kant.

not be a nice balance of advantages, but the living utterance of a Father and a God.

"Hear these three things," said a Jewish Rabbi, "and thou shalt eschew transgression; remember what is above thee, the All-seeing Eye, and the All-hearing Ear, and that all thy actions are written in a book."* But, separated from the thought of God, the conscience becomes an idle enigma. If it do not spring from Him, if it may not appeal to Him, if it cannot testify of Him, it has nothing to say and nothing to command. But herein lies its true supremacy, that it is the voice of that which even the heathen called "the God within us." It is in this sense that St. Paul used conscience; it is in this sense alone that I can understand or speak of it.

2. We have seen then already that the first function of the conscience is *to warn*. And herein is much of its mystery, for it seems to be ourselves, yet not ourselves; inseparable from us, yet no part of us; speaking to us with gentle and divine approval, or with terrible and imperious authority, yet with no inherent power to determine our actions. Wholly beyond our mastery, it stands towards

* *Pirke Aboth*, ii. I.

moral evil in the same relation that pain holds towards disease. When anything is wrong with our bodies, when any function is disturbed, when any mischief is latent, pain comes, whether we will or no, to warn us beneficently of our danger. Nor is it otherwise with the soul. All evil springs from evil thoughts, "out of the heart proceed evil thoughts,"—evil thoughts, and then all the long black catalogue of sins you know. And since an evil thought is, to the soul, a disordered function, an undeveloped disease, a latent leprosy,—when it is lurking there, the pang of an alarmed conscience gives us timely warning. Vain is it to plead that this is but a thought; "Guard well," it says, "thy thoughts: for thoughts are heard in heaven." It was a recognized principle of Roman law that *cogitationis poenam nemo patitur;* but this is not the principle of that sole legislation which had an origin immediately divine. In every other code that the world has ever seen or known, you will find no prohibition of evil thoughts, but you *will* find that prohibition, alike in the first and in the last of those Ten Commandments which are the code of Him, who alone searcheth and knoweth the heart of man. Yea, in the code of heaven, a bad thought indulged is a bad deed committed. Oh if we listen to this warning from the first, if we thus *obstamus principiis*, how strong, how noble, how impregnable to the assaults of evil, may the soul become! For there are but two ways by which men grievously fall, the one is by some sudden access of temptation, the other by the subtle corrosion of some besetting sin. But into the latter, if we be true to that voice within us, we cannot fall, because innocence is nature's wisdom, and conscience faithfully cherished makes it more terrible, more difficult to yield than to resist: and if, on the other hand, evil, unable thus to surprise us by the noiseless and sinuous gliding of the serpent, bounds suddenly upon us with a wild beast's roar and leap, even then it will not master us, because then our habits and our impulses, being pure and true, shield themselves instantly under the strong breastplate of righteousness, and the reiterated choice of what was good has prepared the whole instinct of our nature, the whole bias of our character, for resistance to the sudden sin.

Whatever be the shape that the vile allurement takes, the spirit within us thrills its glad response to the noble utterance of the stainless

Hebrew boy, "How can I do this great wickedness, and sin against God?"

Yes, my brethren, this is the state at which we all should aim:

> "This is the happy warrior,—this is he
> Whom every man at arms should wish to be."

For when we have attained this state, or are attaining to it, then we are happy. Then the eye being single, the whole body is full of light. We reverence ourselves; films fall away from our eyes; we *know* that righteousness tendeth to life; we cherish in our consciences the eternal protest against everything that can degrade and ruin us, the eternal witness that everything sweetest and noblest is within our reach. It is one of the very finest and deepest sayings of the great sage of China that "Heaven means Principle." With him, with all good men who have ever lived, this was the solid result and outcome of experience. Other sources of happiness are but as transient gleams of sunlight, but this is life eternal; other blessings fade as the flowers fade, but this is an everlasting foundation. How full is all Scripture of this one lesson! With what a glow of belief, with what a force of conviction, do those divine utterances crowd upon us, "Blessed is every one that feareth the Lord: oh well is he, and happy shall he be." "The Lord ordereth a good man's going, and maketh his way acceptable to himself." "Thou wilt shew me the path of life; in Thy presence is the fulness of joy; at Thy right hand there are pleasures for evermore."

3. And why, my brethren, do we not all live to inherit this blessedness of which we are all the rightful heirs? Because, alas! we have not all, and not always, listened to that voice of conscience, and not to listen to it is misery; for when it ceases to warn, it begins to *accuse*. The angel who went forth so gently and tenderly at first, to stop us on the path of ruin because our way was perverse, assumes the drawn sword and gleaming robe of the Avenger. And if, in spite of this, we drive with furious passion over the opposing power, as the wicked queen of legend, urging her chariot over the murdered body of her sire, agitated by all the furies, drove through the city with her chariot-wheels all dyed in blood,—then, shamed for a time, and defeated, and defied, conscience, when it speaks

again, speaks in an altered tone; no longer in tones of calm and love, but of sadness and reproach, of scorn and menace, of wrath and fear. And then begins that misery of a *concordia discors*, that *displicentia sui*,* that jangled dissonance in what should be the sweet music of men's lives. "The good that I would I do not, but the evil that I would not that I do." We know the story of how the great king before whom the preacher had been contrasting the misery of these two lives in one, exclaimed, "*I know those two men.*" And indeed this loss of all unity in our being, this miserable disharmony in life, this changing of an inseparable companion from a loving friend into a bitter enemy, this disintegration and dissolution of an existence dragged on in a weakness that still yields while the moral sense would still resist, —the fact that a man should know what he is, and scorn what he is, and yet be what he is, —the sense of an ideal missed, of an opportunity wasted, of all life shrivelled into a miserable "if" and an empty "might have been;"—this is the very essence of human misery. It is man

* Sen. *De Tranq. An.* ii.

without God, and therefore man without joy, or peace, or hope. All Scripture is full of it. The sinner hides himself in vain amid the garden trees, and the sounding footstep follows him, and the awful voice asks, "Where art thou?" He has murdered some mortal body, or worse perhaps, some immortal soul, and it asks, "Where is Abel thy brother?" He has indulged in some secret sneer, or unuttered blasphemy, and setting aside his vain denials, it sternly says, "Nay, but thou didst laugh." He has in his selfish greed made excuses for disobeying some positive command, and it asks, "What meaneth this bleating of sheep in mine ears?" He has stolen what is not his own, and it convicts him with the accusation, "Tell me now what thou hast done." He has committed deadly and undiscovered crimes, and it cries with uplifted voice and threatening finger, "Thou art the man." He has been profane and blasphemous, and while his knees knock together, and his cheeks grow pale, in letters of flame it writes, "Mene, Mene, Tekel" upon his walls. Why proceed? is not all history, is not all experience, full of these haunted men, men pursued by guilt unrepented of, men for whom the whole earth is of glass; men who thought that when the crime was over they had done with it, but who have found that it has not done with them; men who fancied that they had but written their sins on sand, and find them engraved on their own sad memory as with a pen of iron on tablets of brass, and perpetuated in the eternal records "like a crack in the living rock" for ever? No power, no rank can screen them. On the very judgment-seat they are judged. Pilate may wash his guilty hands, but what river can wash his guilty heart? Felix sits on his pompous tribunal, with the scowling lictors on either side, but as Paul reasons of temperance and judgment, Felix trembles. Henry of Germany cowers before the aged Pontiff, who bids him appeal to God's judgment to clear him of his crimes. Sigismund is on his royal seat before all the princes and prelates of this empire, but when the humble priest whom he is about to condemn to the stake reminds him of his broken oath, there, in the presence of them all, he cannot repress the deep blush which dyes his cheek with guilty crimson. There is no peace, saith my God, to the wicked. How can it be peace,

"Nocte dieque suum gestare in pectore testem?"*

How can it be peace,
   "to ever bear about
   A silent court of justice in himself,
   Himself the judge and jury, and himself
   The prisoner at the bar ever condemned,—
   And that drags down his life?" †

No! conscience is her own avenger. "To groan too late over a lost life," ‡ oh what a misery is there! From every age, from every literature, from every history, one might establish it. If the testimony of Scripture be suspected or despised; if those magnificent chapters in the Wisdom of Solomon be thought too akin to Scripture to be accepted, shall I summon the unsuspected, the natural testimony of Pagan witnesses? Shall it be the great poet-philosopher, Lucretius? § "The scourge, the executioner, the dungeon, the pitchy tunic,— even though these be absent, yet the guilty mind with anticipating terror applies the goad, and scorches with its blows." Shall it be the great epic poet who places the *Ultrices Curae* in closest proximity to the *mala mentis gaudia?* Shall it be the youthful satirist, who asks, "Is the moaning of him who is tortured in the Bull of Phalaris;

* Juv. *Sat.* xiii. 198.   † Tennyson, *Sea Dreams.*
‡ Lucr. iii. 1024.   § Ibid.

is the sword that glitters a-tremble over his flushed neck from the gilded fretwork, half so terrible, as

> 'Imus,
> Imus praecipites quam si sibi dicat, et intus
> Palleat infelix?'" *

Or once more, shall it be his fellow-satirist, who exclaims, "Why shouldst thou think that they have escaped, whom the inward consciousness of guilt agitates with amazement and scourges with the soundless lash, *occultum quatiente animo tortore flagellum?"* †

4. But bad as this is, there is something worse than the warning, worse than the accusing, worse than the gnawing,—it is the *dead* conscience. "It is wonderful to observe," says a great bishop of our church, "what a great inundation of mischief will in a very short time overflow all the banks of reason and religion. Vice first is pleasing, then it groweth easy, then frequent, then habitual, then confirmed: then the man is impenitent, then he is obstinate; then he resolves never to repent, and then"—I pause at language which the 17th century was less afraid than the 19th is to use—then comes what comes hereafter. Yes the timid becomes first

* Pers. *Sat.* iii. 39. † Juv. *Sat.* xiii. 195.

the wilful, then the willing sin: πονερὸς, ἀλλὰ τοῦτο ἠὲν καὶ βούλεται.* For what was first tampered with, then yielded to, then persisted in, is next justified; and last, oh horrible, boasted of: aye in whole philosophies, in whole literatures, shamelessly glorified. And this is the stage worse than the gnawing, for this is the *murdered* conscience. When there is any hope for a wound it continues to give pain: but when it has mortified the pain ceases. Even so ceases the throb of a conscience which is sleeping, which is defiled, which is dead, which, in the powerful image of St. Paul, is "seared with a hot iron." For either its voice grows fainter and fainter, as the voice of temptation grows louder and louder, or becoming hateful by its reiterated condemnations, it so inflames the sinner's anger, that he deliberately silences, chokes, murders it. And then he is let alone. His conscience will cease to torment him. And then he may go on undisturbed for years and years, filling to the brim the cup of his iniquity: for years and years he may be dishonest, a drunkard, an adulterer, a

* Aristoph. *Eq.* 1281.

blasphemer: and never once hear again the voice that he has stifled. Nay more, he may, such is the mystery of iniquity, and because it is God's decree that "the more we know of sin, the less shall we feel its real nature," * he may actually substitute for conscience *another* voice; a voice not true but lying, not faithful but traitorous; a voice which, answering him according to his idols, dissimulates the taunting mockery with which it cries, "Go up to Ramoth Gilead and prosper;" a voice that palliates, that excuses, that encourages, that whispers continually, "Peace, peace," when there is no peace. And this is the most perilous of all. It comes to all in proportion to their guiltiness, in proportion to their insincerity. I have known it alas, come even in early years. And it is wellnigh beyond man's cure. Woe to the traveller who turns his back upon the guiding star, that

* This is a profound remark of Mr. J. Martineau. This condition of the soul is called ἀπολίθωσις by Epictetus, *i. e.* "moral petrifaction."
It is the ἀδόκιμος νοῦς (Rom. i. 28), the πώρωσις τῆς καρδίας, best described by St. Paul in Eph. iv. 17-19. See Harless, *Christian Ethics*, E. Tr. p. 92.

he may plunge after the delusive meteor which flickers hither and thither over the marsh of death. Woe to the ship whose pilot, disregarding the friendly beacon, chooses rather to steer by the wrecker's deadly fire. And woe, woe, double woe to that unhappy soul, which wilfully accepts the suggestions of sin and Satan, as though they were the pure, the unerring, the awful voice of God ! *

5. For in this state, with a dead conscience, the man himself may die, and perhaps often does die, his soul as stupefied as the senses of the traveller who lies down to sleep his last sleep on the fields of snow. But sometimes the task of the conscience is even yet not over, and even the murdered starts up once more as the terrified, the awakened conscience. Yes, sometimes for a man's punishment only, but sometimes also by God's infinite mercy, that a man may be saved by that fiery agony, the dead conscience leaps up into angry and terrible life once more, casts off the cerements which years

* σοφία ἐπίγειος, ψυχική, δαιμονιώδης. Jam. iii. 15. σαρκική. 2 Cor. i. 12.

of sin have bound around it, and starts, as the ghost of some murdered victim might start from the tomb, to upbraid its murderer.* Some terrific calamity, some overwhelming bereavement, loss, failure; some arrow of God winged with conviction; some lightning flash, shattering to pieces the smooth path of life, cleaving its way irresistibly into the stony heart, hurling to the ground with a great crash the idols within it; worst of all, some sin becoming the natural punishment, the inalienable possession of sin, some "tempting opportunity" meeting the "susceptible disposition," and leading to some great crime which, though it be but the legitimate issue of a long train of lesser sins, yet startles a man into a recognition of his own awful wickedness, and filling the dark chambers of the heart with a glare of unnatural illumination, reveals the moral law once more in all its insupportable majesty, —something of this kind wakens even the dead conscience as with the trump of the Archangel and the Voice of God. "*Perfecto demum scelere,*

* "It may be obscured," says Tertullian, "because it is not God: extinguished it cannot be, because it is from God." (*De Anim.* xli.)

magnitudo ejus intellecta est." * By that great visitation conscience is awakened. She lights the torch of memory at that lurid glare, and waves it round the painted imagery of the desecrated soul. She is no longer the gentle friend, the soft-voiced monitress, the kind reprover; but she is the executioner with uplifted voice and outstretched arm; the Erinnys with snaky tresses and shaken torch. The man's name is no more Pashur, but Magor Missabib, "terror on every side." And then the maddened soul, tormented in this flame, rushes forth into the night; too often, alas, like Judas into the midnight of remorse and of despair,—into the cell of the madman and the grave of the suicide; but sometimes also, blessed be God, into the night indeed like Peter, but it is to meet the morning dawn.† Then though the Angel of Innocence have long vanished, the Angel of Repentancetakes him gently by the hand. Gently it leads the brokenhearted penitent before the tribunal of his better self, and there his

* Tac. *Ann.* xiv. 10. Cf.
        Quid fas
  Atque nefas tandem incipiunt sentire, peractis
    Criminibus. Juv. *Sat.* xiii. 238.
† Lange, *Leben Jesu.*

old sin, his old weakness, his old pride, his old will is doomed to that death of godly sorrow which even at the eleventh hour may issue in a new and nobler life, and may once more change conscience from a source of terror into a source of perfect and inalienable peace.

6. But how if the conscience never does awake? How if the sinner die rich and increased with goods, and there be no bonds in his death, but only at the evening-tide when there is no light, there peals from heaven, too late, the dread and sudden voice, "Thou fool, this night," and so his dream be broken? What is a dream, my brethren? Is it not to take the substance for the shadow, and the shadow for the substance? the transient for the real, and the real for the transient? time for eternity, and eternity for time? Such a dream is the life of sin. And how if it be broken—not by calamity, not by repentance, not even by remorse—but by the cold clear light of eternity flashed suddenly upon the closed and dreaming eyes; revealing all things in their true proportions, revealing all things in their absolute reality; revealing all things "in the slow sure history of their ripening;" revealing all things as they are, not under the glamour of sensual illusion, not

under the colorings of a treacherous philosophy, not through the distorting mists of a self-deceiving skepticism: but as they are under the pure Eternal Eyes of the Living God? A man has been known in his dreams to walk in perfect safety on the edge of a giddy precipice: but let something disturb that unwholesome slumber,—some light unknown to the sunless cavern of his own dreaming phantasy, some voice which is not a mere dull echo of the impressions from within,—there is a sudden start, a wild scream, a white robe whirling through the air, and he is killed. The dream ends, but it ends in death: the waking certainty begins, but it begins in the Eternal World. Ah me, so may it be when the chill dayspring of eternity falls first in all the clearness of its agonizing reality upon the glaring night of man's illusions! " Like a dream when one awaketh !" were it not better to awake to reality, to be sensible of peril and folly, before the dream and the life are o'er?

I have been speaking, my brethren, before a great University, and some may think that I have spoken on too simple and plain a theme. But in an age when so many deny that God is, and so many more that He is the rewarder of them that diligently seek Him, is it indeed too simple and too plain a theme, to call attention to one of His Voices, to appeal for its reality to the facts of man's experience? If, as a recent writer has truly said, conduct be two-thirds of life,—if respecting so much that occupies even a good man's thoughts we should rather pray, "Oh turn away mine eyes lest they behold vanity, but quicken Thou me in Thy law,"— if the audience of a great University be, after all, composed mainly of youthful souls engaged, as I believe that all of you are engaged, in the hard struggle of life, and the hard endeavor to do that which is right in the sight of the Lord,—and if, again, the helping of one immortal soul to gain the victory over an evil self, and fulfil the true law of its being, be a better and a greater thing than to construct ten thousand ingenious Theodicaeas, or subtle systems of moral Philosophy,—then *are* these thoughts too simple? Are they simpler than Christ preached to the multitude on the green hillslopes, or John on the scorching strand? The language of apology sounds ill on the lips of a minister of Christ. Better say frankly and at once that you must look for no feats of intellect or sophism here. The religion we preach was the religion, not of the disdainful or the cynical, but of the poor and the simple-hearted. It was proclaimed in the loneliness of the desert and nursed in the squalor of the catacomb: the sunrise of its first day flushed over the manger, and the sunset of its last will fall red upon the cross. To you therefore I speak not as wise, or learned, or subtle, or profound, but as a human soul to human souls, as a dying man to dying men. The wind of heaven blows through the frail and feeble reeds, and the voice of the preacher may to some ear be the voice of God to-day. And if but one here feel that on his soul is the burden of iniquity or the stain of guilt, if he be suffering the conscience-stricken misery of a disintegrated and self-despising life, then let me point him to the foot of that cross where alone the burden can be removed, and the stain be washed away. While you are impenitent I know well that you cannot be happy, but rather like the troubled sea that cannot rest: but I point you thither where there is comfort for the wretched, rest for the anxious, peace for the troubled, purity for the defiled. You can find it in Christ; you can find it in the religion which Christ came to teach; you can find it nowhere else. Lose your faith in this, and sin has no known saviour, nor guilt any possible expiation. Oceans of lustral water will not cleanse, nor the burning of hecatombs of sacrifice atone for it, though kindled with the blazing forests of a thousand hills. Lose your faith in this, and then for the troubled conscience there is no peace; not in poppy or mandragora or all the drowsy syrups in the world. Since time was, suffering humanity has been saying to each Prophet in turn,—

> "Canst thou not minister to a mind diseased
> And with some sweet oblivious antidote
> Cleanse the stuffed bosom of that perilous stuff
> Which weighs upon the heart?"

And the answer of all others must be "No;" but the answer of your Redeemer is "Come unto me and I will give you rest." This is the sum of all, that I have striven to say to you. The voice of your conscience is the voice of your God. Obey it, and you will find peace and holiness: disobey it, and you will lose the light of God's countenance, until you repent and learn to obey once more. But to repent heartily is to be forgiven wholly. Yes, I preach to you once more the forgiveness of sins, that forgiveness purchased by the precious blood of Christ. He alone can give peace to the accusing, to the gnawing, to the terrified ; He alone can wake the sleeping conscience, and call it into life again when it is dead. "Neither is there salvation in any other: for there is none other name under heaven given among men, whereby we must be saved." "I have lived," said the wise and gentle Hooker on his deathbed, "I have lived to see this world is made up of perturbations, and have long been preparing to leave it, and gathering comfort for the dreadful hour of making my account with God. And though I have, by His grace, loved Him in my youth, and feared Him in my age, and labored to have a conscience void of offence towards God and towards man: yet if thou, O Lord, be extreme to mark what is done amiss, who can abide it? And therefore, when I have failed, Lord, shew mercy to me ; for I plead not any righteousness, but the forgiveness of my unrighteousness, for His merits who died to purchase pardon for penitent sinners."*

* Walton's *Life of Hooker*, ad fin.

III.

THE VOICE OF HISTORY.

The heathen make much ado, and the kingdoms are moved; but God hath shewed his voice, and the earth shall melt away.—Ps. xlvi. 6.*

So far, my brethren, I have endeavored to engrave yet more deeply upon our hearts the all-pervading and unalterable conviction that God, our God, our Father, our Creator, is a *living* God; that He is not far from every one of us; that His will is the sole intelligible law of our lives; that, if at any time He seems to be silent, that silence is not in Him, but in our own deafness and self-will; that, if our life be true life at all, in Him we live, and move, and have our being. It is a truth of infinite importance, because with it I know of nothing so glorious, without it of nothing so despicable and insignificant as man. "What is man?" asks David in the 8th Psalm, after he had been gazing on the heavens which broke over his head into their immeasurable

* Preached before the University of Cambridge, May 11, 1873.

depth of stars;—and because he feels that He who made those heavens is his Father and his friend, he answers in a burst of exultation, "Thou madest him a little lower than God, thou crownedst him with glory and honor:" but when, in some flushed moment of victory, David again asks in the 144th Psalm "What is man?" then, in the midst of human malignity and human meanness, thinking only of man *without* God, he sorrowfully answers, "Man is like a thing of nought;"—and immediately afterwards, as though in a burst of incontrollable disgust at the crew of liars and blasphemers by whom he is surrounded, he cries, "Cast out Thy lightnings and tear them; shoot forth Thine arrows and consume them:"—feeling as all the best men have ever felt, that when God is with us we may rejoice in "the glories of our birth and state," but that man when he forgets, man when he loses, much more man when he abnegates his God, is a creature so petty, so foolish, so ephemeral, so infinitely to be pitied, that, unless his whole race can be purified by baptisms of fire, it were almost better that it should cease to be.

If then we would rise to the full grandeur of our being, if we would live worthy of our immortality, let us bend our sternest efforts, let us strain our noblest faculties, let us absorb our entire beings in this one aim, to see God's face, to hear His voice, to do His will. And since we have considered how He speaks to us in Nature, which is the translucence of His energy; in the Moral Law, which is the epitome of His will; in Conscience, which is the voice of His Spirit; in Scripture, which is the revelation of His Son;—let us try to-day to mark how He speaks to us also in History, which is "the conscience of the human race," and which has never been more adequately described than as "the prophetical interpreter of that most sacred epic of which God is the poet, and Humanity the theme."

If, my brethren, man were the abject thing to which modern materialism would degrade him, History would have no significance. It would be but like a lamp hung at a ship's stern as she is driven by chance winds over a shoreless sea,—warning of no peril, lighting to no anchorage, only flinging its ghastly lustre over a white wake of wandering foam. But, when we believe, as we *do* believe, that man is a member of Christ, a child of God, an inheritor of the Kingdom of heaven; then indeed the history of man becomes a noble study; it becomes a chapter in that book of Revelation which enables us to recognize in the ways of God an order at once immutable and divine. He who can believe that the story of nations is but a confusion of whirling machinery which no spirit permeates or guides must indeed despise it as an old almanac, or an agreed-on fable; but in this respect the ancient histories were more religious than many of the modern,—from the Διὸς δ' ἐτελείετο βουλή of the mighty Iliad, down to the fine remark of Polybius that "History offers the highest of education, and that it alone, without injury, teaches us from every season and circumstance to be true judges of what is best." One great historian indeed of antiquity is doubtful and gloomy. "I can come," he says, "to no certain conclusion as to whether the affairs of men are guided by the immutable law of destiny, or by the whirling wheel of chance."* And yet it is evident that the whole leaning of Tacitus was towards the nobler faith, and if he seems to waver, it is only because he confined his view to too limited a range. Fallen on very evil times, encircled like our own great poet with the barbarous dissonance of an abominable age, gazing only on the sunset of Roman liberty as its

---

* Tac. *Ann.* vi. 22. Cf. iii. 18, *H.* i. 18, etc.

orb sank slowly into seas of blood, he judged of man's destiny rather as a biographer than as an historian.

But a biographer may easily mistake the middle for the end, and fail to see that the apparent discord in the organ music is not, and cannot be, its close. We read the lives of the saints of God, and we are perplexed at first and saddened to observe how one after another may seem to have perished brokenhearted and despised. One may be slowly torn to pieces like Fra Dolcino, and another may be tortured and strangled like Savonarola, and another burnt like Huss, and another driven to say with the undaunted Hildebrand, "I have loved righteousness and hated iniquity, and therefore I die in exile," and another may faint to death in chilling anguish like Xavier upon the lonely shore: but let us not also fail to notice, that one and all, amid defeat and dishonor, and desertion, they never lose the beatific vision and the transcendant hope: one and all they stretch forth their hands in glorious anticipation of the farther shore. Let us neither be deceived nor saddened by such books as that great recent work of fiction, which shews to us the hopeless failure of so many human ideals, and the chilling sadness of so many human lives.* True, that the *loftier* the ideal, the more complete may seem to be the failure; and the more unselfish the purpose, the more sad the life. In *seeming*, not in reality. Each high ideal is a prophecy which, later if not sooner, brings about its own fulfilment. No good deed dies: be it a rejoicing river, be it but a tiny rill of human nobleness, yet, so it be pure and clean, never has it been lost in the poisonous marshes or choked in the muddy sands. It flows inevitably into that great river of the water of life which is not lost, save—if *that* be to be lost—in the infinite ocean of God's Eternal Love. And it is their intuition of this truth which makes the Idylls of our great poet truer than the fictions of our great novelist. The blameless king murmurs indeed, amid the broken soliloquies of his last troubled night,

> "I found Him in the shining of the stars,
> I saw Him in the flowering of His fields,
> But in his ways with man I found him not:"

yet he never doubts of his mission, or wavers in his purpose. The harp that has been prostituted and jangled on earth shines still among the stars, and to the greatly innocent, and to the sincerely penitent,

* *Middlemarch.*

and to the angels up in heaven, its music is still undisturbed.* And so, as the king dies deeply wounded on the misty shore, yet the bark which carried him vanishes away into the light, "and the new sun rose bringing the new year."† Yes, this is the true and eternal lesson. Ask all good men who have ever died even in bitterest failure whether they would not scorn either to fear or change, and would they not answer with godlike unanimity, " Is not the life more than meat, and the body than raiment?" We sought the struggle not the victory, the service not the reward. Though He slay us yet will we trust in Him; but we have no fear ; He will not slay us; He, the faithful God, who keepeth covenant, will not fling us aside like broken implements, or mock us with delusive hopes ;

"Whoso has felt the Spirit of the Highest
Cannot confound, or doubt Him, or deny:
Yea, with one voice, oh world, though thou deniest,
Stand thou on that side; for on this am I."

If then we fail at times to see this truth in the little facts of our own lives, let us look beyond them, and see it writ large upon the history of nations. What would a man know of the sea by standing but

* *Tristram.* † *Morte d'Arthur.*

an hour or two beside its waters in some small bay? could he suppose that there was anything but idle chance in its little eddies or sweeping currents amid the windings of the shore, as it is fretted by chance puffs of wind, or sways over great beds of seaweed, or is torn by protruding rocks? But let him study the phenomena of the whole great deep itself, and then he will learn with what magnificent and unerring regularity the moon sways the tidal march of those mighty waters which, as they roll onwards, majestic and irresistible whether in ebb or flow, refresh and purify the world. Nor is it otherwise with History. A physical accident, a criminal ambition, a misinterpreted despatch, nay, even the changing of a wind, the stumbling of a horse, the depression of an omen, may seem to have influenced the fortune of nations: but these are, in reality, but eddies and bubbles on the surface of the advancing or receding tide; and, if not in our threescore years and ten, yet in the long millenniums of history, we see the great tidal waves of retribution overwhelming every nation which forgets the eternal distinction of Right and Wrong,—we hear that voice of seven thunders which every true historian has always heard, proclaiming aloud that "for every false word and unrighteous deed, for insult and oppression, for lust and vanity, the price has to be paid at last. Truth and justice alone endure and live. Falsehood and injustice may be long-lived, but doomsday comes to them in the end."

Yes, every great historian should be no dull registrar of events, but a prophet, standing, like him of old, amid the careless riot and luxurious banqueting of life, and teaching men to decipher that gleaming message of God, written, as with the fingers of a man's hand, on the parliament of nations and the palaces of kings, that what is morally just must be politically expedient, that "what is morally wrong cannot be politically right." And in doing this the Hebrew prophets have been our truest teachers, nor have any teachers ever enforced that great lesson with such divine insight, with such unalterable certitude, with such passionate intensity as they. Around their little insignificant strip of plain, and hill, and valley, towered the colossal kingdoms of a cruel and splendid heathendom; but to their enlightened eyes these, in their guiltiness, were but phantoms on their way to ruin, casting a weird and sombre shadow athwart the sunlit horizons of a certain hope. What matter their force, their splendor, their multitude, if they stand before the slow-moving chariot of the Eternal God? Is it the Kenite? "Strong is thy dwelling-place, and thou puttest thy nest in a rock; nevertheless the Kenite shall be wasted." Is it Assyria? "The Lord, the Lord of Hosts, shall send among his fat ones leanness, and kindle under his glory a burning fire." Is it Egypt? Her wise magicians shall be smitten with fatuity, and the papyrus of her rivers fade. Is it golden Babylon, the city of the oppressor? The dead, moved at his coming, ask her king with gibbering taunts, "Art thou also become weak as we? art thou become like unto us?" Is it purple Tyrus with her priceless merchandise? "Take a harp, go about the city, thou harlot, that hast been forgotten." And so with all. "The nations shall rush like the rushing of many waters, but God shall rebuke them; and they shall flee far off, and shall be chased as the chaff of the mountains before the wind, and like a rolling thing before the whirlwind. And behold at eveningtide trouble; and before the morning he is not." "This," exclaims the prophet in a flame of triumphant zeal, "this is the portion of them that spoil us, and the lot of them that rob us."

Thus over the heads of the enemies of Israel did her prophets roll, like a Pyriphlegethon of living fire, the denunciation of God's wrath on sin. Never had any nation been taught that lesson as Israel had been taught it, from the fearful eloquence of the maledictions upon Ebal, down to the days when Isaiah wailed his dirge over " Ariel, the Lion of God, the city where David dwelt." Nor had they been taught by words alone. When Israel was yet a child God loved him, and out of Egypt He called His son. In the Old Testament we see that son grow up to life. Many were the sins, the follies, the apostasies of his youth. Can you point me to one folly which was not visited with its natural consequences? to one pleasant vice which did not become its own punishment? to one sin which was not lashed with its own appropriate scourge? Then came the ruinous and crushing humiliation of the Babylonish Captivity. A remnant, which they themselves compared but to the chaff of the wheat, returned; and of the old temptation, the temptation to a sensual idolatry, they were cured for ever. But they were not saved from other sins. Keeping the form of their religion they lost its spirit; from a living truth they suffered it to degenerate into a meaningless ritual, into a dead formula, into a hypocritical sham. They had for centuries been hoping, dreaming, talking of a Messiah, and their Messiah came; and how did they receive Him? they received Him with yells of "Crucify." And there, in Scripture, at the Cross which consummated their iniquity, the story of their nation ends. But History, which proves the responsibility of nations, History adds its chapter to the Sacred book. It shews how soon the wings of every vulture flapped heavily over the corpse of a nation that had fallen into moral death. Some of those who had shared in that scene, and myriads of their children, shared also in the long horror of that siege which, for its unutterable fearfulness, stands unparalleled in the story of mankind. They had shouted, "We have no king but Cæsar," and they *had* no king but Cæsar, and leaving only for a time the grotesque phantom of a local royalty, Cæsar after Cæsar outraged and pillaged them, till at last their Cæsar slaked, in the blood of his best defenders, the red ashes of their desecrated Temple. They had forced the Romans to crucify their Christ; and they were themselves crucified in myriads by the Romans outside their walls, till room failed for the crosses, and wood to make them with. They had preferred a murderer to their Messiah, and for them there was no Messiah more, while a murderer's dagger swayed the last counsels of their dying race. They had accepted the guilt of blood, and the last pages of their history were glued together with that crimson stain; and, to this day, he who will walk round about Jerusalem sees in its ever-extending miles of gravestones and ever-lengthening pavements of tombs and sepulchres, a vivid emblem of that field which Judas bought with the price of his iniquity,—a potter's field to bury strangers in, an Akeldama, a Field of blood.

2. I turn from Judaea to the short but splendid tragedy of Athenian history; how short, how brilliant, how terrible, you all know well. Yes, we owe to Greece an infinite debt of intellectual gratitude. The exquisite ideal of beauty of her race, the grace, the subtlety, the activity of her intellect, the perfection and supremacy of her art, the power and splendor of her literature, conferred upon her a wreath of unfading admiration. O had she but learned righteousness; had she but won the grace to obey, as she had received the insight to read that law written upon the fleshy tablets of her heart! But

she chose otherwise; and now the world may learn as memorable a lesson from the rapidity of her fall, and the utterness of her extinction, as from all besides; for the ever-needed moral of that little hour in which she played her part upon the lighted stage is this, that intellect without holiness, beauty without purity, eloquence without conscience, art without religion, insight without love, are but blossoms whose root and life are in the corruption of the grave. All these gifts combined saved her not from being eaten away by that fretting leprosy of her favorite sins, which degraded the Μαραθωνομάχης of her youthful glory into the *Graeculus esuriens* of her consuming degradation. With what fearful sternness was the career of Athens cut short! It was but ninety years after her handful of heroes had clashed into the countless hosts of Persia and routed them, that her walls were razed among the songs and shouts of her insulting enemies. Some who had seen the one might have seen the other. And when the hour of her ruin came, when, on that sleepless September night of terror and agony, down the long walls from the Peiraeus to the Acropolis rang that bitter unbroken wail which told that the fleet of Athens had been destroyed at Aegospotami;

it is one of her own sons who tells us that it was
the shameful consciousness of her former tyrannies;
it was the avenging memory of Melos, and Torone,
and Scione, that made that bitter hour more bitter
still, by bidding her remember that even-handed
Justice was but commending to her own lips the in-
gredients of that poisoned chalice which in the plen-
itude of her pride and selfishness she had forced
the weak, and the defeated, and the unfortunate to
drink.* A great lesson doubtless, but the real
lesson of Grecian history is deeper, more universal,
more permanent than this; and surely in days
when some men, in the worst spirit of the tainted
and godless renaissance of the fifteenth century, are
beginning shamelessly to preach a corrupt Hellen-
ism, which regards sin forsooth with æsthetic tolera-
tion,—in days when we have read the thoughts of
one calmly arguing an ideal so wretched and so base
as that it is best to crowd life with the greatest
number of pleasurable sensations,—in days when
hearing has been found for theories of an artistic
effeminacy, which, one hopes, would have made even
Antisthenes and Epicurus blush,—it is time, I say,
to read again that stigma of infamy which the

* Xen. *Hell.* ii. 1, 2.

Apostle branded for ever on the unblushful forehead of the paganism which he saw, that its sons "became vain in their imaginations, and their foolish heart was darkened;" that it was God Himself who gave them over to vile affections, and to a reprobate mind, because, "knowing the judgment of God, that they which do such things are worthy of death, they not only did the same, but had pleasure in them that did them."

3. Take but one more prominent example from ancient days to shew that there is no distinction between the sacred and the secular, and that profane history is sacred too. From the palsied hands of Greece, Rome rudely snatched the sceptre. And you know that so long as the character of Rome was simple and self-respecting; so long as her family life was pure and sweet; so long as she was the Rome of the Camilli, the Cincinnati, the Fabii, the elder Scipios; so long as her dictators came from the honest labor of the ploughshare, and her consuls from the hardy self-denial of the farm, so long she prospered till none could withstand her, and impressed the world with lessons of law and order and discipline manlier and better than any which Greece had taught. But, when the dregs of

every foreign iniquity poured their noisome stream into the Tiber; when the old iron discipline had yielded to an effeminate luxury and a gilded pollution; when her youth had grown debased, and enervated, and false; when all regard had been lost in her for man's honor and woman's purity; when her trade had become a flagrant imposture and her religion a dishonest sham; when, lastly, her literature became a seething scum of cynicism and abomination such as degrades the very conception of humanity,—then you know how justly, in long slow agony, the charnel-house of her dominion crumbled away under the assaults of all her enemies, and

"Rome, whom mightiest kingdoms curtsied to,
Like a forlorn and desperate castaway,
Did shameful execution on herself."

And why did that giant power fall into fragments before the weak hands which held a despised and hated cross? Why? because, and only because, God is King; because in the long run there is nothing fruitful but sacrifice; because it is self denial not luxury, humility not insolence, love not violence, justice not ambition, which overthrow the world.

4. And that Christian Church, why was it that

it too fell from that splendid eminence to which by the immense ascendancy of justice, and the faith in Eternal Laws, it had attained in the days of a Hildebrand, and an Innocent? What was it but crime after crime that dashed the Papacy into dishonored ruin? The boundless ambition of Boniface VIII., the greedy avarice of John XXII., the shameful violences of Urban VI., the unblushing nepotism of Sixtus IV., the execrable crimes of Alexander VI., the aggrandizing wars of Julius II., it was not till the disgusted nations had long been alienated by such spectacles as these that a humble monk of Erfurdt, rising in the irresistible might of moral indignation, shattered the supremacy of the Vatican for ever. I might go on with history; I might ask why Spain, once the Lady of Kingdoms, is now the most despised and impotent of European powers; I might ask what changed the strong and righteous England of the Commonwealth, to the nation which suffered a perjured trifler to sell Dunkirk, and live in infamy on the subsidies of France; I might ask how comes it that at this very day our beloved English Church, working as she is now beginning so heartily to do, amid the hatred of her opponents and the disunion of her sons, may, even yet

be unable to escape, by her late repentance, the
Nemesis of falling axe and kindled flame due to the
sluggish impotence and truckling worldliness of her
18th century. But though time forbids this, I
ought not to take all our instances from the past
when one flagrant illustration of this great truth
has happened in the present, and under the very
eyes of the youngest here. Is there, I ask, no plain,
no unmistakable lesson in the collapse and catastrophe of modern France? Warnings enough she
had received; warnings of splendor overwhelmed
with darkness, warnings of strength smitten into
decrepitude, warnings of defeat, warnings of mas-
sacre, warnings of revolution, from the day when
her great monarch so sadly confessed to the little
child " I have loved war too much " to the day
when, in the living tomb of St. Helena, her imperial
conqueror had time to meditate on his audacious
blasphemy—" men of my stamp do not commit
crimes." But as fast as she had received such lessons, she had, alas! forgotten them. Her religion
had become a godless materialism; her practice a
calculated sensuality; her literature a cynical jour-
nalism which sneered at every belief, and a leprous
fiction which poisoned every virtue. She trusted

in her armies, in her numbers, in her prestige, in the *élan* of her soldiers, in the *persiflage* of her journalists, in the vaporing patriotism of her *boulevards*,—in anything and everything save in God and right. And what came of it? Her magnificence melted away like a vision of the Apocalypse; her unfortunate Emperor became a despised, broken idol; like the corpse of some exhumed king, her strength slipped into ashes at a touch. And the causes of this were too obvious to miss. They lay in her puerile vanity, her administrative corruption, her universal effeminacy; they lay in the bourgeois materialism which desired nothing but vulgar luxury; in the absence of all dignity and seriousness in the old, and of all discipline and subordination in the young.* These sorrowful accusations are taken not from the indictment of her enemies, but from the confession of her sons: they are from a book of a member of her Institute. "Tainted all of us," says another, "in the depth of our hearts, we must disengage ourselves from our habits, from our morals, from our facilities, from our conventions of yesterday, to reascend to the primitive sources of numanity and ask ourselves simply but resolutely

* Renan, *La Réforme intellect, et morale, passim.*

the question—Is it right, distinctly Yes or No, that there should be a God, a morality, a society, a family? ought woman to be respected? ought man to toil? Is truth the end; is justice the support; is the good absolute? Yes, yes, a thousand times Yes! And societies, governments, families, individuals, can they, if they would be noble, durable, fruitful, do without these conditions? No, no, a thousand times No." * Such was the lesson of the late prostration and calamity of France, read not by me but by one of themselves, even a prophet of their own; by one who has done his best to help the corruption he deplores, and whose very name I can hardly mention here. And yet, so little has it been learnt, that I read how but a few days ago one of her most prominent statesmen asserted, amid the applause and laughter of his audience, that God permits the existence of so many iniquities that He cannot be regarded as of much account in estimating the progress of the world ! †

* Alex. Dumas, fils, *Une Lettre sur les Choses du Jour*, p. 30.
† " These gentlemen declared that they acknowledged no controlling power but God and their conscience. As for the former of these powers, it has permitted so many iniquities to be perpetrated that its invocation cannot be said to have much influence in human affairs " (applause and laughter). From a *Times* report of one of M. Gambetta's speeches.

This then is the law, this the philosophy of History. And it not only is but must be so, because the will of God governs the universe, and God's will is the moral law.

And therefore all unrighteousness is sin, and all sin is, necessarily, weakness. You will not, I am sure, ask me what you have to do with all this? what the history of nations has to do with you? It has everything to do with every one of you. For each biography is but a fragment of history; each soul but an epitome of the world. Nations are but aggregates of such as you; and Universities are no small part of a nation's life; and if this University send forth, year by year, men who are brave, because their consciences are clear and their hearts are pure; if, year by year, Cambridge add to the life of England her stream of youthful students who are manly, and soberminded, and fearless, and faithful, then she will be adding no small momentum to the forces which keep England great. But, on the other hand,

> " Vain mightiest fleets of iron framed,
> Vain those all-conquering guns,
> Unless proud England keep untamed
> The true heart of her sons."

Your lot is cast in stirring and not untroubled

times. Before you die there will have been many a vast change in the constitution of society, and many a battle of God will have been lost or won. Oh may you fight on God's side! Fight against greed, fight against falsity, fight against faithlessness, fight against uncleanness in your own hearts, and so shall you be ready for all God's work both now and any time hereafter, until your Master gives you the signal that you may fall out of the ranks, or it is time for you, not as men might say in their despair, to give up their broken swords to Fate the Conqueror, but to yield your pure souls to your Captain Christ. Then, whatever happens, your life will not have been in vain; then having heard His voice here you shall be with Him hereafter, and you shall say, as you stand, with bowed head indeed and awful reverence, but yet a forgiven and an accepted child before that unutterable glory,—you shall say, with such joy as here the heart of man cannot conceive, "I have heard of Thee by the hearing of the ear, but now mine eye seeth Thee."

IV.

WHAT GOD REQUIRES.

Wherewith shall I come before the Lord, and bow myself before the high God? shall I come before Him with burnt offerings, with calves of a year old? Will the Lord be pleased with thousands of rams, or with ten thousands of rivers of oil? shall I give my firstborn for my transgression, the fruit of my body for the sin of my soul? He hath shewed thee, O man, what is good; and what doth the Lord require of thee, but to do justly, and to love mercy, and to walk humbly with thy God?—MICAH vi. 6–8. *

WHEREWITH shall I come before the Lord, and bow myself before the Most High God? It is indeed a momentous question, the most momentous that can be framed in mortal words. For as we enter deeper into the valley of life, and its rocks begin more and more to overshadow us, to what do all the other questions of life reduce themselves? To any man who has the slightest sense of Religion, —to any man, who, with all his imperfections, yet solemnly feels that if life is to be life at all, every year must bring him nearer and nearer to the great

* A Lent Sermon, preached at the Chapel Royal, St. James's, February 16, 1872.

Light,—to all whom the sorrows and disappointments of life have for ever disenchanted,—no hope, no thought, no question remains but this, Is God's love with me? Am I at peace with Him? In one word, am I His? Oh! if not, how shall I, the lowliest of His creatures—how shall I approach Him? What else can I care for but this? Remove the fear of God's displeasure, and I have no other fear. Give me the joy of His countenance, and I ask no other joy. Whatever may have been the illusions of youth, they have vanished from the eyes of manhood. The winds have carried those bubbles beyond the river, or, as we seemed to touch them, they have burst; but one thing have I desired of the Lord, that will I seek after, even to behold the fair beauty of the Lord, and to visit His Temple. Wherewith then shall I come before the Lord, and bow myself before the Most High God?

Many and various, in all ages, have been the answers to that question, but in spirit and principle they reduce themselves to the three, which in these verses are tacitly rejected, that the fourth may be established for all time. And, therefore, this is one of those palmary passages of Holy Writ, which should be engraved on every instructed conscience as indelibly as by a pen of iron upon the living rock. It formulates the best teaching of religion; it corrects the worst errors of superstition. Every book of Scripture, every voice of Nature, every judgment of Conscience re-echoes and confirms it. Happy will it be for us, if we will use it as a lamp to guide our footsteps, a law to direct our life.

(1) The first answer is, Will Levitical sacrifices suffice? "Shall I come before Him with burnt-offerings, with calves of a year old?" that is, "Shall I do some outward act, or acts, to please God?" Men are ever tempted to believe in this virtue of *doing* something; to ask, as they often asked our Lord, "What shall I *do* to inherit eternal life?" And there are times when such external systems may, for ignorant and stiff-necked nations, be a wise safeguard. It was so for the Israelites at the Exodus, depressed and imbruted as they were by long slavery, and saturated with heathen traditions of cruelty and vice. The Levitical institutes,—so multiplex, so trivial, so intricate, so material, so burdensome,—statutes which were not good, and judgments whereby they could not live,—were best suited, intolerable as was their yoke, to a people which in honor of their brute idol, could sit down to eat, and

to drink, and rise up to play, while the body of heaven in its clearness had scarcely vanished from their eyes, and the majesty of darkness still rolled around the burning hill. There have been attempts in all ages to revive such ceremonials, or others like them, because they are easier than true holiness, and tend to pacify and appease the perverted conscience. But God's own Word about them is plain; they perish in the using; they cannot sanctify to the purifying of the flesh; nay, in so far as they are substituted for a heart religion,—in so far as they are used to compound for the weightier matters of the law,—in so far as they furnish an excuse for selfishness, for censoriousness, for party spirit,—they are eminently displeasing to God. External observances, without inward holiness, are but the odious whiteness of the sepulchre. "Bring no more vain oblations, incense is an abomination unto Me," saith God to such; "your sabbaths and calling of assemblies I cannot away with." Thousands, I suppose, have been asking themselves this Lent, Need we fast? Yes, my brethren, if you think that you ought; and if you know and find that by doing so you increase your religious earnestness, and strengthen your moral life. But not if you think that fasting is an end instead of a means ; not if it renders you more self-satisfied ; not if it makes you less active in works of good ; not if it renders you less lenient to your own failings. "Eat an ox, and be a Christian," said the Jesuit Fathers to a penitent who could not abstain from meat. What is the passionate, indignant language of the Prophet Isaiah on this subject? "Behold, ye fast for strife and debate, and to smite with the fist of wickedness: is it such a fast that I have chosen? to bow down his head as a bulrush, and to spread sackcloth and ashes under him? wilt thou call this a fast, and an acceptable day to the Lord?" No: fasting may be necessary, only do not take it for religion;—but, on the other hand, look at home ; loose the bands of wickedness, your own and others; undo the heavy burdens, your own and others ; take the beam out of your own eyes ; wash you, make you clean ; put away the evil of your doings from before Mine eyes; cease to do evil ; learn to do well. That is dearer in God's eyes than perpetual sacrifice, holier and purer than days of unbroken fast.

(2) If then we cannot please God by merely doing, can we by *giving?* "Will the Lord be pleased with thousands of rams, and ten thousands

of rivers of oil?" Shall we like the Pagans try to bribe God? Shall we make His altars swim with the blood of hecatombs, and fill his sanctuaries with votive gold? Or shall we, like terrified sinners in the Middle Ages, think to buy off his anger by bequeathing our possessions to charity or to the Church? Ah! my brethren, I suppose that while not one of us is so ignorant as not to know the duty of charity, none of us is so exquisitely foolish as to imagine that he can by gifts win his way one step nearer to the great White Throne. Sacrifices, to bribe Him whose are all the beasts of the forest, and the cattle upon a thousand hills? Gold or gems to Him, before whom the whole earth, were it one entire and perfect chrysolite, would be but as an atom in the sunbeam? Ah, no!

> "Vainly we offer each ample oblation;
> Vainly with gifts would His favor implore;
> Better by far is the heart's adoration,
> Dearer to God are the prayers of the poor."

"Thou desirest not sacrifice, else would I give it Thee, but Thou delightest not in burnt-offerings. The sacrifices of God are a broken spirit; a broken and a contrite heart, O God, Thou wilt not despise."

(3) If then neither by doing, nor by giving,

can we please God, what third experiment shall we try? shall it be by *suffering?* Shall I, lacerating my heart in its tenderest affections, give my firstborn for my transgression, the fruit of my body for the sin of my soul? This, too, has been frequently and fearfully attempted; frequently, and fearfully, and more persistently than any other, because in all ages, and in all nations, men have invested God with the attributes of terror and of wrath. Could we, my brethren, judge rightly of the glorious sun in heaven, if we only saw it glaring luridly through the whirled sands of the desert, or dimmed and distorted by the hideous ice-fogs of the North? And can we, my brethren, judge of God—the Sun of our souls—when He looms dark and terrible through the crimson mist of haunted consciences and guilty hearts? No; when men have been able only to thus regard Him, then all the day long His terrors have they suffered with a troubled mind. He, the All-loving, the All-merciful, has seemed to them cruel, wrathful, irresistible, delighting in smoking victims and streaming blood. And thus alike in sunny Greece, and stately Rome, and apostatizing Israel, and scorching Africa, and in the far sweet islands of the sea, to hideous emblems of some savage Deity,

—a Moloch, an Odin, an Atua, a Sheeva,—in the rushing stream, or the molten furnace, or on the blade of the consecrated sword, has the blood of man been shed in abominable sacrifice, or his life robbed of all health and joy in horrible self-torture. Nothing seemed too sanguinary or revolting to appease the sense of sin, or dim the glare of awakened wrath.

> "Our sires knew well
> The fitting course for such; dark cells, dim lamps,
> A stone floor one may writhe on like a worm,
> No mossy pillow blue with violets."

They fled from the society of their fellows to vast wildernesses, or desolate hills, or wave-washed caverns. Knowing their sin, not knowing their Saviour,—gazing in remorse and tears at the splendors of Sinai, not coming in humble penitence to the Cross of Calvary,—life became to them an intolerable fear. When a man feels that the eye of God is fixed upon him in anger, and knows not how to escape, then no mountain seems too heavy, no sea too deep, no solitude too undisturbed. He says with the poet,

> "Place me alone in some frail boat
> Mid th' horrors of an angry sea,
> Where I, while time may move, shall float
> Despairing either land or day.

> Or under earth my youth confine
> To the night and silence of a cell,
> Where scorpions round my limbs may twine,—
> Oh God! so thus forgive me Hell."

But has any man ever found these sufferings sufficient? Has any man ever testified that he found forgiveness through voluntary torture? Or is not that true which is said of the prophets of Baal, "They leaped upon the altar, and cried aloud, and cut themselves after their manner. And it came to pass that there was neither voice, nor any to answer, nor any that regarded?"

(4) Not then by doing, not by giving, not by suffering may we come before the Lord, or bow ourselves before the most high God. Oh! if we could thus be at peace with Him, who would not be doing incessantly, who would not give all that he has, who would not cheerfully suffer, as never martyr suffered yet? Yet let us not imagine that if men have acted thus in sincerity, it will all have been in vain. No, let us take comfort, knowing that God is love. Though not by any number of formal actions can we enter into eternal life, yet no work done from a right motive, however erroneous, can be the fruit of an utterly corrupted tree. Though no self-inflicted anguish can be acceptable to God, yet "agonies

of pain and blood shed in rivers are better than the soul spotted and bewildered with mortal sin." Though no giving shall purchase interest in heaven, yet the poorest and slightest act which has sprung from a true charity,—the kindly word spoken in Christ's name, the cup of cold water given for His sake,—shall not miss its reward. You may remember how, in the old legend, St. Brendan, in his northward voyage, saw a man sitting upon an iceberg, and with horror recognized him to be the traitor Judas Iscariot; and the traitor told him how, at Christmas time, amid the drench of the burning lake, an angel had touched his arm, and bidden him for one hour to cool his agony on an iceberg in the Arctic sea; and when he asked the cause of this mercy, bade him recognize in him a leper to whom in Joppa streets he had given a cloak to shelter him from the wind, and how for that one kind deed this respite was allotted him. Let us reject the ghastly side of the legend, and accept its truth. Yes, charity—love to God as shewn in love to man—is better than all burnt-offering and sacrifice. Yet if we condemn the errors of other ages in their mode of approaching God, let us at the same time humbly remember that, better had we be at ceremonials all day long,—better be giving in the most mercenary spirit of self-interest,—better even be a Moloch worshipper, drowning with drums the cries of his little infant as he passes it through the fire,—than to be a Christian living, as alas! so many live, without God in the world; living in pride, fulness of bread, abundance of idleness ; living, while they are unjust, unmerciful, uncharitable, unholy, in self-satisfied pharisaism, in gluttonous indifference, in sensual ease.

Yet if all these be at the best but unacceptable ways, what is the true way of pleasing God? If not by doing, not by giving, not by suffering, then how? What is the Prophet's answer? My brethren, by *being*. "He hath shewed thee, O man, what is good ; and what doth the Lord require of thee, but to do justly, and to love mercy, and to walk humbly with thy God?" Not once or twice only in Scripture are we taught the same great lesson. "Behold," said Samuel to the presumptuous king, "behold, to obey is better than sacrifice, and to hearken than the fat of rams." "I spake not to your fathers concerning burnt-offerings," said Jeremiah, "but this thing commanded I them, Obey my voice." Four times over,—thrice to the murmuring Pharisees, once to the inquiring Scribe who was not far from the kingdom of heaven—did our Lord expressly sanction the same high principle. By *being* then shall we please God; but by being what? By being correct in the pronunciation of half-a-dozen shibboleths? By being diligent in a few observances? By fasting? By attending Church services? By saying "Lord, Lord," when, all the while, the heart is unsanctified, the lips uncharitable, the passions unsubdued? No, my brethren, no a thousand times; but by being just, and merciful, and humble before our God. It is the answer of all the Prophets, it is the answer of all the Apostles, it is the answer of Christ Himself. Justice that shall hate the wicked balances,—justice that shall recoil from oppression and violence,—justice that shall loathe the small vices of gossip, scandal, and spite:—mercy that shall make us careful

"Never to mix our pleasures or our pride
With anguish of the meanest thing that feels;"

mercy that shall cherish for every sorrow which can be alleviated, and every pang that can be assuaged, a divine, trembling, self-sacrificing love; mercy which, looking neither to be admired, nor honored, nor loved, shall live for the good of others, not its own;—and lastly, a humble reverence towards God, which shall be the source alike of that high justice, and that heavenly mercy,—oh this is what God requires, and thus alone can we live acceptably to Him. Yea, acceptably; for this is to live in Christ. In Him was justice fulfilled; in Him was mercy consummated; in Him was such humility of reverence towards His heavenly Father that, alike on the hills of Galilee, and in the garden of Gethsemane, we see Him absorbed in constant prayer. Oh! my brethren, God needs not our services; He needs not our formulæ; He needs not our gifts; least of all does He need our anguish; but He needs us, our hearts, our lives, our love; He needs it, and even this He gives us; shedding abroad the spirit of adoption in our hearts. If we resist not that Spirit we need no longer be what we are; no longer what we have been. All meanness and malice, all deceitfulness and fraud, all injustice and insolence, all pharisaism and uncharity, all worldliness and lust will fall away from us, and we shall be clothed, as with a wedding garment which Christ shall give, with justice, and humanity, and purity, and love. Oh! if we would indeed know how to serve Him aright, let us put away all idle follies and fancies of our own; and seating ourselves humbly at his feet, amid those poor and ignorant multitudes who sat listening to Him among the mountain lilies, let us learn the spirit of his own beatitudes — *Blessed are the meek for they shall inherit the earth; blessed are the merciful for they shall obtain mercy; blessed are they that hunger and thirst after righteousness for they shall be filled.*

V.

AVOIDANCE OF TEMPTATION.

Then the devil taketh Him up into the holy City, and setteth Him on a pinnacle of the temple, and saith unto Him, If Thou be the Son of God, cast thyself down: for it is written, He shall give His angels charge concerning Thee: and in their hands they shall bear Thee up, lest at any time Thou dash Thy foot against a stone. Jesus said unto him, It is written again, Thou shalt not tempt the Lord thy God.—MATTHEW iv. 5–7. *

THIS which is the second temptation in St. Matthew is, as you are aware, the third in St. Luke. It may be that the younger Evangelist, looking upon it as a temptation subtler and more perilous than any which could come from earthly splendor, regarded it as the *last* because it was the *deadliest* assault. But the fact that St. Matthew alone gives us definite notes of sequence,—the fact that, as an actual Apostle, he is more likely to have heard the narrative from the lips of Christ Himself,—the fact that the recorded words, "Get thee behind Me,

* A Lent Sermon, preached in Hereford Cathedral, March 7, 1872.

Satan," seem to be the natural conclusion of the entire temptation, render it all but certain that the order of the actual temptation was that which the first Evangelist adopts.

Nor is this all; for there is also in this order an inherent fitness, a divine probability. It represents, on the part of the tempter, a Satanic subtlety of insight, which the acutest human intellect could hardly have invented. For our Saviour had foiled the first temptation by an expression of absolute trust in God. Not even the pangs of famine in the howling wilderness would tempt Him one step aside from the perfect confidence that His heavenly Father *could*, and, in His own time, *would* prepare for Him a table in the wilderness. Adapting himself therefore with serpent cunning to this discovered mood of the Saviour's mind,—breathing a suggestion which must seem but the natural sequel of that triumphant faith,—the tempter challenges this perfect trust, not to gratify an immediate need, but apparently to avert an immediate peril. There is no stain of egotism, no impatience of suffering, in the present temptation. Transformed therein into an angel of light, the tempter breathed his insidious suggestion as a sublime victory of Messianic power, a striking illustration of sovereign faith. Transporting the Saviour to the Holy City, where

> "The glorious temple reared
> His pile far off,—appearing like a mount
> Of alabaster, tipped with golden spires,"

the tempter set Him not on *a*—but as it should be more accurately rendered—on *the*—on the *topmost* pinnacle. Probably it was the summit of that Stoa Basilikè, or Royal Porch, which towered over the southern extremity of the magnificent mass. At this point the walls of Jerusalem surmount a rocky and elevated platform; and as the porch itself was of stupendous height, we are told by the Jewish historian, no one could gaze down from it into the sheer descent of the ravine below without his brain growing giddy at the yawning depth of the abyss.

"If thou be the Son of God;"—again that whispered doubt as though to challenge Him through spiritual pride into an indignant exercise of His miraculous power,—"If Thou be the Son of God, cast Thyself down." Is not this Thy Temple, this Thy Father's house? Here the prophets prophesied about Thee; here Anna and Simeon took Thee in their arms; here, while yet a boy, Thou didst amaze by Thy wisdom the teachers of Thy people.

And here, save Thyself, or, if not save, at least assert Thyself by the splendor of miracle, in the majesty of faith. Give to every passer in the valley a sign from Heaven. Flash down, like a star from the zenith, amid the astonished populace. Art Thou afraid? Nay, for—(and here mark how well the devil can quote Scripture for his purpose, and set the fatal example so greedily followed, of isolating, perverting, distorting Holy Writ)—for "He shall give His angels charge concerning Thee: and in their hands they shall bear Thee up, lest at any time Thou dash Thy foot against a stone."

So deadly subtle, so speciously plausible, was this second temptation. There was nothing vulgar in it, nothing selfish, nothing sensuous. It seemed all spiritual; and oh! to how many a Pharisee, and Reformer, and Saint, have such and similar temptations proved a fatal snare! But calm, spontaneous, deep with warning, came the simple answer, "It is written again, Thou shalt not tempt the Lord thy God!" The word in the original is yet stronger,— it is, οὐκ ἐκπειράσεις, thou shalt not *tempt to the full*, thou shalt not challenge to the extreme—the Lord thy God; thou shalt not wantonly experiment upon the depth of His pity, or the infinitude of His power. When thou art doing thy duty, then, trust Him to the uttermost with a perfect confidence; but let no seductive whisper thrust thee into suicidal irreverence in thy demand for aid. Thus, to add the words omitted by the tempter, shalt thou be safe in all thy ways:

"Also, it is written
Tempt not the Lord thy God: He said and stood;
But Satan—smitten by amazement—fell."

Now no one, I suppose, can ever have meditated even superficially on the Temptation in the Wilderness, without feeling its many-sided and searching applicability; and though, at the first glance, this second temptation may seem merely to involve a spiritual pride, which, if not uncommon, is yet far from universal, I think that if we look at it a little more closely in humble simplicity, we shall, on the contrary, find it full of warning to the youngest, no less than to the oldest, to the worst sinner no less than to the loftiest saint.

The key to its meaning lies surely in the answer of our Lord. It is an allusion to the Book of Deuteronomy, "Ye shall not tempt the Lord your God, as ye tempted Him at Massah." And how had the children of Israel tempted God at Massah? They were in the wilderness, and in lack of water; but hitherto God had guided, had fed, had loved them; for them He had smitten the parted sea; for them empearled with manna the barren waste; for them

> "By day along the astonished lands
> The clouded pillar glided slow,
> By night Arabia's crimsoned sands
> Returned the fiery column's glow."

And could they then, indeed, suppose that God would desert them there to die of thirst? What did they need but a little calm faith, a little patient trustfulness, a little obedient hope, and then assuredly for them should the wilderness have rippled with living waves? But what did they do? They broke into angry murmurs; they clamored with self-willed indignation; they demanded as a right the smiting of the stony rock. This was emphatically to tempt the Lord. It was at once presumption and distrust, distrust of God's ordinary Providence, presumption of His miraculous aid. It was neither faith, nor submission, nor hope; it was rebellion—it was sin.

1. Are we, then, never liable to tempt the Lord our God, as Israel tempted Him in the wilderness, as Christ refused to tempt Him on the Temple pin-

nacle? Yes, in many ways. Christ would not cast Himself down, because He respected, as the laws of His Father, the laws of nature; and to cast Himself down would have been to brave and to violate them. Now, we too, by our knowledge of those laws, by study of them, by obedience to them, are placed as it were upon a pinnacle of the Temple,— on a pinnacle of that vast Cathedral of the Omnipotent, whose azure dome is the vault of heaven, and the stars its cresset lamps. Consider the supremacy of man in nature. For us are fire and hail, snow and vapor, wind and storm; for us are the glorious voices of the mountain and the sea; for us the shell upon the sand has its rosy beauty, and the moon in heaven her silvery light. And look what man has done! How he has made the very elements minister to his happiness, and decrease his toil,—how he has, as it were, seized the very lightning by its wing of fire, and bidden it flash his messages through the heart of mighty mountains, and the bosom of raging seas. But how? *By exact obedience to the laws of nature, never by insolent violation of them.* "The water drowns ship and sailor like a grain of dust; but trim your bark, and the wave which drowned it will be cloven by it, and carry it like its

8

own foam, a plume and a power."* But is there no moral lesson for us here? Aye, and a deep one: for the Book of Nature is also the Book of God, and the Voice of Nature the Voice of God; and the history of man, and the life of man, would have been very different, if—instead of neglecting that Book, being deaf to that Voice, violating those Laws, and so flinging himself down from that Temple pinnacle, whereon his feet are set—he had in all respects and in all ages humbly and faithfully striven to understand and to obey. Half of the peace and prosperity of nations, half of the health and happiness of man, half even of the serenity and security of moral life, depend on this. For pain, mutilation, disease, death — these are the stern, instant, inexorable penalties affixed by nature to every violation of every law. Drop a spark near a magazine, and a city may be shattered; let hot ashes fall in a prairie, and a province may be devastated. The germs of diseases the most virulent, which spread dismay and disaster through nations and continents, lurk in the neglected cottage, and the stagnant pool. And, as you all know, these laws have a direct bearing on the individual life of man.

* Emerson, *The Conduct of Life.*

By obedience to their beneficent indication can we alone preserve a sound mind in a sound body. He who would live to a green old age in purity and honor,—he who would "account himself both a fit person to do the noblest and most glorious deeds, and far better worth than to deject and to defile with such a pollution as sin is, himself so highly ransomed and ennobled to a filial relationship with God,"—he who would not lay waste the inner sanctities of his own immortal nature, or lie down in the dust with his bones full of the sin of his youth,—he must regard the laws of nature as a voice behind him, saying, " This is the way, walk ye in it," when he would turn aside to the right hand or to the left. And then, indeed, he may feel that God's angels shall guard him in all his ways. Never will he

"With unbashful forehead woo
The means of sickness and debility."

The sudden terror, the pestilence of darkness, the arrow of noonday shall have no dread for him. Or if he suffer, he will calmly and cheerfully accept such suffering as a part of God's providence for his mortal life, knowing that *any* suffering encountered for the sake of duty with unflinching courage, endured for the sake of duty with perfect trust, is only less noble than martyrdom itself. It is related of one of the bravest of our kings—a king who, in many a hard fight, when horses were shot under him and bullets tore his clothes, exulted with a serene and imperturbable courage,—that he had yet a deep contempt for foolhardiness and neglect. "What do *you* do here?" he once asked sternly and angrily, of a gentleman who had come to witness a battle. "Do you not see the danger you are in?" "Not in greater danger than your Majesty," was the reply. "Yes," answered the king, "but I am here in the path of duty, and therefore may trust my life in God's care; but you—" . . . before the sentence could be finished a cannon-ball laid the rash intruder dead at the unharmed monarch's feet.

2. Again, *by our spiritual and moral privileges*, no less than by the laws of nature, we stand as it were upon the pinnacle of the Temple. Consider our lofty privileges. We are, every one of us, members of Christ, children of God, inheritors of the kingdom of heaven. In infancy the Cross was signed upon our foreheads; in youth we were taught at Christ's school; in manhood the deepest and richest ordinances of a free and unpersecuted religion were placed wholly within our reach. How many by such

privileges as these have been tempted to their own destruction! "Admitted into the holier sanctuary they have but been guilty of the deeper sacrilege; standing in the brighter radiance they have but flung the deeper shadow." How many, even in the early Church, cast themselves down at the tempter's bidding into the gulf of Antinomianism; how many in all ages have imagined that *they in particular* need not be guided by the strict letter of the moral law. How is all such pride rebuked, how is the eternal majesty and grandeur of the moral law asserted, by Christ's calm answer, " Thou shalt not tempt the Lord thy God." As long, indeed, as we stand firm where His Providence hath set our feet we are secure. " He shall defend thee under His wings, and thou shalt be safe under His feathers; His righteousness and truth shall be thy shield and buckler." Daniel when he prayed thrice a day looking towards Jerusalem was but doing what he had ever done, and therefore for him the lions' mouths were sealed. The three children were but resisting unsought temptation, when they were dragged before the golden image, and flung into the burning flame, and therefore for them the Spirit of God breathed like "a moist whistling wind " amid the fire. But, or the other hand, when the early Christians thrust themselves presumptuously and insolently into the peril of martyrdom, how often did "the flaming inspirations of idealist valor" sink shamefully under the rude shock of reality. And the fall of many of them was more terribly shameful, when they put themselves with reckless self-confidence in the way of moral temptations. As long as men watch and pray, and use the ordinary means of safety furnished by God's grace, so long they are safe; but when they despise those ordinances, how utter may be their ruin! When Lot, in his greed for gold, was willing to exchange his nomad tent for the foul city's wicked streets, how in the shipwreck of all he had and all he loved,—how in the earthquake-shattered city, and the lightning-riven plain,—how in the putrescent scum and glistening slime of that salt and bitter sea, which rolled its bituminous horror where his garden-pastures had smiled before,—how, I say, did he learn that God means even the most innocent-hearted to keep far away from sin! When Dinah walked forth to see the daughters of the land, and returned to bitterness and bloodshed, with rent veil and dishevelled hair;—when Peter followed into the High Priest's palace, and was startled by sneering questions to deny with shameless curses the Lord he loved,—how in their moral feebleness, how in their sudden retribution, do they illustrate the great sin and folly of rushing into danger's way! Yes! *the devil tempts us* when he thrusts sin before us, but, when we approach it of our own selves, it is then *we who tempt the devil;* and " Lead us not into temptation" is a prayer which will not be heard from the lips of him who makes no effort to avoid it. He who walks humbly, prayerfully, watchfully, on the path of quiet duty, may indeed meet with danger; but if so, firmly holding the hand of God,—unshaken, unseduced, unterrified,—he shall tread upon the lion and adder, the young lion and the dragon shall he trample under feet. But he who dallies with temptation, he who tampers with evil, is *never* safe. People say that such and such a man had a sudden fall; but no fall is sudden. In every instance the crisis of the moment is decided only by the tenor of the life; nor, since this world began, has any man been dragged ever into the domain of evil, who had not strayed carelessly, or gazed curiously, or lingered guiltily, beside its verge.

3. Once more and lastly, and this is a point which nearly affects us all, independently of all

spiritual privileges, independently of God's inestimable love in the redemption of the world by our Lord Jesus Christ, we are set as it were upon a pinnacle of the Temple, by the mere grandeur and loftiness of our being, by the freedom of our wills, by the immortality of our souls, by the glory and honor, a little lower than the angels, wherewith God has crowned our race. And how often, alas! and how fearfully, do men fling themselves down from this glory and grandeur, into the abyss!

> "Ah deeper dole!
> That so august a spirit, shrined so fair,
> Should, from the starry session of his peers,
> Decline to quench so bright a brilliance
> In Hell's sick spume;—ah me the deeper dole!"

For, indeed, by every sin,—above all by every *wilful*, by every *deliberate*, by every *habitual* sin,—we *do* fling ourselves from our high station down into shame and degradation, into guilt and fear, into fiery retribution and, it may be, final loss. And yet, how many talk in these days as though to sin were no great harm; as though the sins of youth, for instance, were all venial, and it were rather a better thing than otherwise for a young man to sow, as they call it, his wild oats! But yet, though man deceive himself and be deceived—though the tables of the Moral Law, even ere they were promulgated, were shattered to pieces on the mountain granite—the Moral Law remains in its eternal majesty, and in the heart and conscience of every living man, louder than amid the thunder-echoing crags of Sinai, "*God spake these words and said.*" So that *every* violation of God's law is to fling ourselves down from the Temple pinnacle into the foul and dark ravine ;—it is to see whether man's insolent rebellion shall not triumph over God's immutable designs.

And to what do men trust, to what alas! do *we* trust when we act thus? Is it not to the lying whisper that God will give His angels charge over us, and that, whatever we do, we shall still be saved? But oh, we cannot learn too early that stern lesson of St. Augustine's that though God hath indeed promised forgiveness to those who repent, He hath not promised repentance to those who sin. We cannot convince ourselves too absolutely, that, if we sin, God will work no miracle for our deliverance. People talk of *time* producing a change in them; but time is no agent, and can lend no aid. And thus, more men destroy themselves by hope than by despair; by the hope that is—the vague, vain, idle hope,—that they will some day be saved, than by the despairing conviction that they never can be saved. It has been often said that "hell is paved with good intentions;" it would be far more true to say that hell is paved with idle hopes. Century after century has the tempter been whispering to myriads and myriads of human souls, "Cast thyself boldly down. Yea, *hath* God said?—Fear not! Thou shalt not surely die. Thou shalt enjoy the sweetness of the sin, and shalt escape—for God is merciful—the bitterness of the punishment." And yes, my brethren, God *is* merciful; but shall we make His mercy an excuse for our own wickedness, or pervert His love into an engine for our own destruction? Did our first parents, did any of all their millions of descendants in all ages, ever find that whisper true? In the lost Paradise, in the crushing shame, in the horror at God's presence, in the waving barrier of fire about the Tree of Life, in the son who was murdered, in the son who was a murderer, in the ruin, and anguish, and degradation that burst in like a flood upon their race,—did they find that God thinks nothing of His word, and does not mean what He has said? And if indeed He does not, what mean in history the battles and the massacres, and in nature the earthquake and the pestilence, and in daily experience the cell of the lunatic and the grave of the suicide ? Do these look like "a reckless infinitude of mercy, and boundless obliteration of the work of sin ?" Might we not, it has been said, seeing a river, hope that it is not a river, and so walk into it and be drowned, as seeing, in all Scripture, and in all nature, judgment and not mercy written down as the penalty of impenitent transgression, "hope that it is mercy and not judgment, and so rush against the bosses of the Eternal buckler as the wild horse rushes into the battle ?"

Thus then, my brethren, if Satan tempt us to cast ourselves down from that high pinnacle, whereon we are now standing,—whether it be by neglecting the law of Nature, or by presuming on the law of Grace, or by defying the law of Retribution,— we shall, if we yield to that temptation, be yielding to our own destruction. But to each of such temptations we have the true answer, "Thou shalt not tempt the Lord thy God." Trust Him, but tempt Him not. Trust Him, for thou art His child ; and if thou wilt love and fear Him, the very hairs of thy head are all numbered. In the accidents of life, in its dangers, in its difficulties, in its moral crises, yea, in the very valley of the shadow of death, trust Him; but in obedience, not in rebellion; in faith, not in audacity; in humble patience, not in insolent self-will. So, but so only, shall He give His angels charge concerning thee, and in their hands they shall bear thee up lest at any time thou dash thy foot against a stone.

VI.

THE CONQUEST OVER TEMPTATION.

There hath no temptation taken you but such as is common to man: but God is faithful, who will not suffer you to be tempted above that ye are able; but will with the temptation also make a way to escape, that ye may be able to bear it.—1 COR. x. 13.*

You have just heard these words, my brethren, in the second lesson of this evening's service. They form the climax of a long and memorable digression of which the leading thought is distrust of self, trust in God,—distrust of self as a cause of watchfulness, trust in God as a ground of hope. Like most of St. Paul's words, real and burning words as they always are, they acquire a yet intenser significance from the sequence of thought with which they are connected. He has been speaking of his position as an Apostle, and claiming his right to be supported by his evangelizing work. But he reminds his Corinthian converts that he had deliberately waived that right.

* Preached as a Farewell Sermon in the Chapel of Harrow School on the evening of Jan. 29, 1871.

He had followed that rarer and nobler course which is so hard to learn, and which he urges so often on all Christians, of calmly and habitually being content if need be, with less than is our due. And therefore, instead of accepting the maintenance to which he was so clearly entitled from the hands of his converts, he had labored with his own hands to meet the modest wants of a disciplined and simple life. Yet he did not boast of this great self-denial; he had not done it for glory, or for gratitude, but for God. What he had done he could not help doing. The sacred hunger for souls had absorbed his energies; the burning impulse of love had swayed his soul; his labor had been its own reward, because it had been done for the Gospel's sake, that he and they might alike be partakers of its benefits.

And there for a moment he pauses. The thought arrests his attention. You may have sometimes watched a great tide advancing irresistibly towards the destined shore, yet broken and rippled over every wave of its sunlit fretwork, and liable at any moment to mighty refluences as it foams and swells about opposing sandbank or rocky cape. Such, as the elder of you will recognize, is the style of St. Paul. The word "Gospel,"—the thought of sharing with them its awful privileges,—arrests him; he is suddenly startled at the grandeur of his own mission, and stops to warn them that even he, their teacher,—even he called to be an Apostle,—even he with all his perils and labors and sacrifices, needed, no less than they did, unsparing, constant, anxious self-discipline, lest he should become a castaway. He reminds them that the mortification, the conflict, the self-mastery which were necessary for him who would wear heaven's wreath of amaranth,[*] were far more intense and continuous than the severe training which the young athletes of their city must undergo before they could win those coveted and fading garlands of Isthmian pine. He reminds them too of the awful lesson involved in the history of their fathers. They, by glorious privilege, had been guided by the fiery pillar, had been baptized in the parted sea, had quenched their thirst from the cloven rock,—yet all had been in vain. In spite of all, their hearts had lusted after evil things. Some had committed fornication and fallen in one day three and twenty thousand; some had tempted Christ and been destroyed of serpents; some had murmured and been destroyed of the destroyer. Oh

---

[*] 1 Cor. ix. 25. 1 Peter v. 4. τὸν ἀμαράντινον τῆς δόξης στέφανον.

let them beware, for all this dark and splendid history was written for their example. It was no dim revelation of God's will, no uncertain utterance of His voice. And its lesson was "Let him that thinketh he standeth, take heed lest he fall." But then, at once, after those stern and solemn messages, the heart of the great apostle breaks with tears. He yearns to comfort his children. " Why *should* they—why *need* they fall ? " The thought flashes across his mind too rapidly for utterance, and leaving it unexpressed, he continues, " There hath no temptation taken you but such as is common to man ; but God is faithful, who will not suffer you to be tempted above that ye are able ; but will with the temptation also make a way to escape, that ye may be able to bear it."

At those blessed words, my brethren, *we* too will pause. They are words of mercy, of strength, of confidence, of comfort. Very gladly for a few moments would I dwell on them as my last words amongst you. Very earnestly would I pray to Almighty God, that, as a savor of life unto life, their meaning may linger in our souls ; and that thereby we may be helped forward by God's grace on the path of a Christian life, feeling more peace amidst its troubles, more courage under its difficulties, more hope amid its failures, more joy as the quiet scene of its many blessings gleams forth under the sunlight of God's approving smile.

1. Mark first, my brethren, that St. Paul assumes *the certainty of our encountering temptation.* No life, not even the life of our Lord and Master, was ever yet without it. That journey of the Israelites in the desert to which St. Paul alludes, furnishes a close emblem of our own. Before each one of us—a pillar of a cloud by day, a pillar of fire by night,—glides visibly the protecting providence of God. Wonderful deliverances are vouchsafed to us. Enemies pursue us, and we must fly from them. Enemies confront us, and we must fight with them. Vividly and distinctly, loudly and intelligibly,—as among the burning summits and thunder-beaten crags of Sinai,—blaze for us the revealing splendors, reverberate for us the majestic utterances of the moral law. Simple and sweet as virgin honey, —if we will only live thereon,—lies round us the angels' food; clear and crystalline,—if we will but drink thereof,—murmurs and shines about us the river of God's love. Yet, alas! we fall as Israel fell. Idolaters like them, we inflame ourselves with idols.

Sensualists like them, we sigh for the fleshpots of Egypt among the manna-dews of heaven. Thankless as they, we have been discontented and rebellious in the midst of mercies. The language is allegorical, the fact is bitterly real. All of us have been tempted; many of us have fallen; some have been overthrown in the wilderness.

And these temptations—these impulses from without, these tendencies from within, to love our bodies more than our souls, our pleasures more than our duties, ourselves more than our God,—begin, alas, almost with our earliest years. The very youngest boy who hears me, knows what it is to be tempted to do wrong,—tempted to neglect known duties, to utter wicked language,—tempted to be idle, or self-indulgent, or unholy, or unkind. Ah my brethren, let us not conceal it,—let us frankly acknowledge the plain fact,—an English Public School,—nay, *any* school, public or private, is, and must be a scene of temptation. That temptation may vary in extent, in intensity, in deadliness; at one time, in one house, under one set of circumstances it may be fearfully virulent;—under happier influences it may be comparatively faint;—but it will be always there. It must needs be that offences come. To one who feels the sacredness of life, to one who cares for the souls of others, to one who can thrill with an emotion of assent to that crushing indignation which "flung the desecrator of youthful innocence with a millstone round his neck into the sea," the advent of a new boy to a Public School must always cause anxiety; he must be carefully shielded, gently watched over, wisely, and, if need be, even solemnly forewarned. And even then, though many a prayer be poured forth for him at the throne of grace, though hands firm and tender be outstretched to upbear his stumbling feet, nay, even though, in the silent watches of the night, hours of sleepless thought may have been given to his welfare, as they *have* been given by many here for many here,—he may cause bitter disappointment, he may go terribly astray. My brethren, it is not my purpose to awaken the memories of the past; yet, as I look back over a space of more than fifteen years, it is sadly, solemnly true, that I have known some with whom God was not well pleased, some who, listening to the subtle whispers of temptation, forsook the guide of their youth to perish in the wilderness. I mean not, God forbid! those over whose young graves the grass is green; those whom in the midst of us the voice of God has called, the finger of death has touched. I knew indeed each and all of those whose names, from these mute tablets, make to you their touching and eloquent appeal; I knew many others, whose names are unrecorded here, but whom,—some by the sharp stroke of accident, some down the lingering declivities of disease—God, perhaps only because they were so fit to die, called away to their long home, nearer to their heavenly Father, nearer to their brother Christ. On *their* vacant places we could always gaze without a tear; but from time to time there have been *other* vacant places among you, not due to death; the vacant places of those who once were innocent, who once were simple-minded, who once were upright, but from whom, partly for their own good, partly for yours, it was best that you should separate. And others there have been who have not left us in sorrow; but yet, if you could call them here, —if they could show you how their feet have been lacerated by the thorns which their own careless hands sowed broadcast on their youthful path,—if they could reveal to you what it is to bleed inwardly and well nigh unto death with self-inflicted wounds, —if, saved so as by fire, they could make you feel beforehand that (it may be in years long after) a man must possess and inherit the sins, aye and even the mere follies of his youth,—*then with what emphasis of warning, then with what solemnity of dread, would you hear St. Paul's admonition to distrust of self*,—would you learn that your life here is to all but the careful and the prayerful a time of danger,—that it is a wilderness of temptation in which many fall.

2. Yes, so much I was forced to say; but I add eagerly and joyfully that you *need* not fall,— not *one* of you need fall,—every one of you may become pure, and sweet, and noble; every one of you may die a holy man. My subject is not warning, but comfort; and St. Paul's comfort to those whom he loved was this, " There hath no temptation taken you but such as is common to man." Perhaps you will say that this is no comfort.

> "That loss is common would not make
> My own less bitter; rather more;
> Too common,—never evening wore
> To morning, but some heart did break."

When a ship is going down in the angry sea, is it any comfort to the drowning struggling mariner to think that all his comrades also,—all whom he has honored, all whom he has loved,—are buffeting hopelessly with those overwhelming waves? No, my brethren, the consolations of Scripture are not like this; but how if we could tell him that though *some* will perish, all might escape? How if we pointed him to the life-buoy floating near him on the billows,—to the life-boat straining towards him through the storm? How if, without concealing his peril, yet cheering, aiding, inspiriting the bold swimmer,

> Courage, we cried, and pointed toward the land;
> This mounting wave will roll us shoreward soon?

Aye this is St. Paul's comfort—not that our temptations are common to man, but they are *human;*[*] that there is nothing strange, abnormal, insuperable about them; that they are well within the scope of our power to struggle with. If you would kindle a soldier into daring would you point out to him his spiritless, defeated comrades,—the victorious insulting foe? Would some French general—a Chanzy or a Bourbaki,—cheer on the despairing armies of France in the hour of battle by telling them of the retreat from Moscow or the rout at

---

[*] Greek ἀνθρώπινος A. V. marg. "*Moderate*."

Waterloo? Would he not rather fire their memories with the heroisms of Valmy and of Marengo, with the glories of Jena and of Austerlitz? Would he not tell them how, exhausted by drought and weariness, their glorious fathers had shattered the magnificent chivalry of the Mamelukes at the Pyramids, and how, ragged and shoeless, yet irresistible, they had swept through the storm of fire to hurl the German artillery from the Bridge of Lodi? Even so, in a world of sin and sorrow, in a moral world which has its own disgraces and defeats, St. Paul would point us not to those sad pale multitudes of wasted and ruined lives,—not to the retributive diseases of desecrated bodies, or the gnawing Nemesis of guilty souls,—not to the chain of the felon, or the cell of the lunatic, or the grave of the suicide,—ah no! these with an infinite pity, these with a faith that transcends and tramples on the petty Pharisaisms of dogma, these, sorrowing but not scorning, compassionating but not condemning, we leave with infinite tenderness in the tender hands of God,— but no! *he* points us, and *we* point you now, to the glorious company of the high and noble, of the pure and holy; to the white-robed, palm-bearing procession of happy human souls; to those who have fought and conquered, to those who have wrestled and overcome!

3. But these perhaps you will say to me are the strong great souls, the Scævolas of Christian daring, the Manlii of Christian faith. Temptations insignificant to them might well be insuperable to us. Nay, my brethren, *God is faithful*, and will not suffer you to be tempted above that ye are able. In an age of cold faith and dead enthusiasm no splendid heroisms, no agonizing martyrdoms are required of you. Ye have not yet resisted unto blood, striving against sin. Not yet, like the boy Origen, have you seen a father torn from you by violence; or like the girl Blandina, been called upon to face the cruel gaze of the bloody amphitheatre. He who tempers the wind to the shorn lamb, tempers also the temptation to the weak soul. He knoweth our frame, he remembereth that we are but dust. Oh in that hero-multitude who follow the Lamb whithersoever he goeth, think not that there are only the dauntless and the powerful, the great in heart and the strong in faith: no, there are many of the weak and the timid, many of the obscure and the ignorant, many of the shrinking and the suffering there. We saw not, till they

were unfolded for the flight of death, their angel wings. Yes! Jacob, once a mean trickster, and Aaron, once a weak apostate, is there; and Rahab the harlot, and David the adulterer; and Mary the weeping Magdalene, and Matthew the converted publican, and Dysmas the repentant thief; many as frail, many as fallen, many as sinful as the weakest and the worst of you; but there are no stains on their white robes now; there is no weakness or meanness in their regenerated spirits now, and the solemn agony has faded from their brows. You think that you could never have been a martyr, yet women more timid, and children more delicate, have won and worn that crown; nearer to the flame they were nearer to Christ, and as the balmy winds of Paradise beat upon their foreheads while the fire roared about their feet, so believe me will it be with you. I have known martyrs here—boys ungifted and unattractive, boys neglected and despised,—yet so firm in their innocence, so steadfast in their faith, that no evil thing had power to hurt them. Every day their struggle was easier; every day their path more happy. Weak, unloved, and singlehanded, they overcame the world. And why? Oh, if any passing interest attaches to the accident of these last words, would that I could leave you this thought as an indelible impression;—Why? because *God is faithful.* To us in our blindness, ignorance, waywardness, He does not always seem so. To the strong man when he sits, despairing and stricken, amid the ruins of his life,—to the father whose erring son causes him agony and shame,—to the mother who kneels broken-hearted beside the cradle where her pretty little one lies dead,—to these the sun shines not, and the stars give no light,— the heavens above their heads are iron, and the earth beneath their feet is brass. Yet, oh how gently He heals even for these the wounds which His own loving hand has made ; how do the clouds break over them and the pale silver gleam of resignation brighten into the burning ray of faith and love. Why art thou so cast down, oh my soul, and why art thou so disquieted within me ? Trust thou in God. Is there one of you, is there one in this chapel whom he has not richly blessed ? I am sure that there is not one of you. For our path in life, my brethren, is like that of the traveller who lands at the famous port of the Holy Land. He rides at first under the shade of palms, under the golden orange-groves, beside the crowded fountains, with almonds and pomegranates breaking around him into blossom: soon he leaves behind him these lovely groves; he enters on the bare and open plain; the sun burns over him, the dust-clouds whirl around him; but even there the path is broidered by the quiet wayside flowers, and when at last the bleak bare hills succeed, his heart bounds within him, for he knows that he shall catch his first glimpse of the Holy City, as he stands weary on their brow. Oh how often, my brethren, must the Christian, in this the Holy Land of his short pilgrimage on earth, from the golden morning to the blaze of noon, from the burning noon to the beautiful twilight, again and again recall that tender verse of the Prophet, "I know the thoughts that I think towards you," saith the Lord, "*thoughts of peace and not of evil.*"

4. Yes, God is faithful; and most of all, because He will lay no heavier burden on any one of us than we can carry well. Whether in the way of trial, or in the way of temptation, remember, my brethren, in the words of the poet,

> " 'Tis one thing to be tempted, Escalus,
> Another thing to fall."

We shall all be tempted, but the effects of the

temptation depend upon ourselves. Fling into the same flame a lump of clay and a piece of gold,— the clay will be hardened, the gold will melt; the heart of Pharaoh hardened into perfidious insolence, the soul of David melted into pathetic song. Bear temptation faithfully, and it will leave you not only unscathed, but nobler. With each temptation God will also provide not—as the English version has it—*a* way, but *the* way of escape;* the one separate escape for each separate temptation. Because God loves us, because Christ died, because having risen again He shed forth the Spirit in our hearts, therefore under the fiercest assaults of Satan the soul may be always safe. It may be like a beleaguered city, the powers of evil may marshal all their devilish enginery, and make the air hiss with their fiery darts, but every sortie of the besieged shall be inevitably successful; never shall there be capitulation; and by true resistance the assaults of the tempter shall at last be driven back in irretrievable, disgraceful rout.

It would take me too long, my brethren, were I to dwell on *the* way of escape from each temptation.

* ποιήσει σὺν τῷ πειρασμῷ καὶ τὴν ἔκβασιν.

But without dwelling on them, I would gladly mention—and merely mention—four, with the power and efficacy of which I have been often struck. i. The first is *watchfulness over the thoughts.* As is the fountain, so will be the stream. Quench the spark, and you are safe from the conflagration. Crush the serpent's egg, and you need not dread the cockatrice. Conquer evil thoughts, and you will have little danger of evil words and evil ways. The victory over every temptation is easiest, is safest, is most blessed there. ii. The second way is *avoidance of danger.* The best courage, believe me, is sometimes shown by flight. Consider which is your weakest point, who are your most dangerous companions, which is your guiltiest hour. Avoid those companions, defend that weak point, put the strongest guard upon those hours. iii. Then, thirdly, *overcome evil with good.* Kill wicked passion by religious passion. Expel evil affections by noble yearnings. Banish mean cravings by holy enthusiasms. "*Give me a great thought,*" said the German poet, "*that I may live on it.*" Read great books; enrich your minds with noble sentiments; above all, read your Bibles; fill your whole souls with the thought of Christ; make of him not only a Redeemer, but a brother,—not only a Saviour, but a friend. iv. And fourthly, I will mention *prayer*. That, my brethren, is the truest amulet against the siren songs, the holiest enchantment against each Circæan spell. Suffer me to quote the words of that great poet, whom I have wished many of you to love:

> "Amongst the rest a small unsightly root,
> But of divine effect, he culled me out;
> * * * * *
> He called it Hæmony, and gave it me:
> And bade me keep it as of sov'ran use
> 'Gainst all enchantments, mildew, blast, or damp,
> Or ghastly furies' apparition."

I have said nothing, my brethren, of happy Sabbath days; nothing of the strength that comes from mutual communion; nothing of these delightful services; nothing of kindly admonitions; nothing of confirmation; nothing of the memories of baptism; nothing of that divine viaticum on life's journey, the Supper of the Lord. My brethren, I cannot say all I would, or a tithe of all. Would to God that this little might be enough; enough to convince you that because God is faithful you never need do wrong; enough to point to the drawn sword in the path of wilful sinners; enough to show to those who are struggling timidly that around them are angel champions, and over them are invincible shields. To those who are new boys among you, I would say, Resist the devil, and he will flee from you. *Obsta principiis*—avoid the beginnings of evil—this is *the* way of escape for you. And you who have learnt here some lessons of sin and sorrow, believe me that no less to you also lies open the way of escape. Oh rouse yourselves, and play the men. Indolence and selfishness would terrify you by the sight of lions in the path, but press onward and you will find them chained. God does not mean you to perish. Your Lord came to seek the sinful; He died to save the lost. Make but one effort, and yours too shall be the blessedness of Him "whose iniquity is forgiven, whose sin is covered."

My subject is ended. I thank God from my heart that it has been a subject of comfort, of encouragement, of hope. And here I would gladly close, but the last word must be spoken however painful. After more than fifteen years among you, it would not be natural, you would not wish me, to make no allusion to a parting which to me at least is very full of pain. Yet what shall I say? To those Colleagues who for so many years have treated me with such generous sympathy and indulgent kindness, I would offer from a full heart my sincere and earnest and grateful thanks. To all those— not a few of your number—whom at one period or other it has been my high privilege to teach, I would say, if God has ever enabled me to speak to you any true and righteous words, continue thou in the things that thou hast learned. To those who have been placed towards me in the yet nearer and dearer connection of Friends and Pupils, I would say, Think kindly of me still, and for my sake think and speak kindly of the new home to which God's providence is calling me. And on all the Masters and Scholars and Benefactors of this great and famous school I would invoke God's richest and choicest blessings. You are entering on a year of intense interest. I pray to God that the tercentenary of Harrow may be right royally prospered; and when its celebrations are over, when its benefits are achieved, may it witness the yet deeper blessing of ever holier traditions; may it hand on from year to year the ever-brightening torch of knowledge and of truth. But one word more. When the last echo of my voice shall have died away, we shall all kneel upon our knees to utter in silence one last petition ere the Sabbath services are over and we leave the House of God. Oh suffer me to beg of you, as my last request, that each one of you, Masters and Boys and Friends, would, as you kneel before our common Father, utter one brief prayer for God's blessing upon him whose place here will know him no more. It will cheer me more than I can tell you in the midst of new and difficult reponsibilities, to think that, as I was leaving my Harrow home, the hearts of all in this School Chapel which we love so well, were for one moment united as the heart of one, in the sweet and peaceful petition "For my brethren and companions' sake I will wish thee prosperity ; yea, because of the house of the Lord our God I will seek to do thee good."

τ δεῷ Οεῷ χάρις τῷ διδόντι
ἡμῖν τὸ νῖκοσ διὰ τοῦ Κυρίου ἡηῶν
'Ιησου Χριστοῦ.

VII.

WISDOM AND KNOWLEDGE.

Wisdom is the principal thing: therefore get wisdom: and with all thy getting get understanding.—PROVERBS iv. 7.*

READ in the light which falls upon it from the teaching of Christ and His Apostles, there is, perhaps, no Book of holy Scripture which illustrates more clearly than the Book of Proverbs the objects and the privileges, the duties and the dangers, of this seat of learning. Into the wonderful structure of that book, into the πολυποίκιλος σοφία of its noble teaching, it is not my purpose to enter; but there are two features of it which will immediately strike the most careless reader; one is the allusive contrast which runs through its earlier chapters, the other is the constant connection of Wisdom with Knowledge. Two voices are heard in it,—the voice of Prudence and the voice of Folly ; the voice of Virtue and the voice of Pleasure ; the pleading of the vir-

* Preached in the chapel of King's College, London, at the Annual Commemoration, July 16, 1871.

gin Innocence and the pleading of the harlot Sense; the enticements of a Passion earthly, sensual, devilish, and the lofty invitations of a Wisdom which is pure, peaceable, gentle, full of mercy and good fruits.

Subtle, and sweet, and perilous, and evanescent, —powerful only to the soul that forgets its God,— heard only in the twilight, in the evening, in the black dark night, an unhallowed song is suffered to break in upon those solemn utterances; a song, drowned almost from the very beginning by the groans of the deluded and the stern epitaph pronounced over the living dead: and ever, overmastering that strain, shaming it into terrified silence, chilling it into penitent despair—is heard that other Voice, pure as the voices of the Seraphim, offering peace and pleasantness in life, and hope and safety beyond the grave,—an ornament of grace for the living, a crown of everlasting remembrance and unfading glory for the dead.

And while the praises of this heavenly Wisdom are painted in such fair colors,—while its worth is set far above rubies and crystal, the gold of Ophir, and the topaz of Ethiopia,—it is, both in the Book of Proverbs and in other parts of Scripture, united constantly with Knowledge. "In the night that God did appear unto Solomon, He said unto him, Ask what I shall give thee. And Solomon said unto God, Give me now wisdom and knowledge. And God said unto Solomon, Wisdom and knowledge is granted unto thee." They are not mere synonyms. Knowledge may come when wisdom lingers; and, on the other hand, wisdom may exist in rich and divine abundance where knowledge is scanty and superficial. And it is clear that, in Scripture, wisdom is the loftier and the more sacred of the two. Take knowledge to mean the sum total of every magnificent endowment and every extensive acquisition; —let it involve not only erudition, but insight; not only information, but intellect; not only theoretical acquaintance, but practical ability; make it include, if you will, the power to think as Plato thought, and to write as Shakespeare wrote; bestow it on one single mind with such brightness as never yet illuminated the world, and reward it with a splendor of reputation such as no man ever yet enjoyed,—yet even then knowledge falls far, far below wisdom,—below wisdom merged in obscurity; below wisdom accompanied by ignorance; below wisdom burdened with every earthly calamity, and insulted by every human scorn. Does not all history justify herein the estimate of Scripture? Have we not read of men whose heads towered high above their contemporaries, who by eloquence, or song, or intellect, have elevated and charmed mankind, and yet of whom the humblest child, the most ignorant pauper in the kingdom of heaven, is greater than these? Any age will furnish us with examples. Seneca uttered words of lofty morality and almost Apostolic force, yet his inconsistent sycophancy and grasping avarice awoke the scorn of even a dissolute and greedy age. Abélard was endowed with an intellect keener than is granted in a century to any of our race; yet so flagrant was his folly, so fatal his vanity, so gross his crime, that the miserablest could afford to look on him with pity, and almost the meanest with contempt. Bacon has won for his glorious intellect the reverence and admiration of every succeeding age, yet there is, alas! many an ignoble passage of his life which can only claim to be forgotten by the generous, and forgiven by the just. Has not God over and over again scattered penal blindness over vaunted acquisitions, and smiting a godless intellect with a moral imbecility, has He not frustrated the tokens of the liars, and made diviners mad? But why need we dwell on the fact that intellectual eminence is no preservative against moral infatuation, when God has written the same truth so large over the history of nations? Have we not known mighty peoples who, professing themselves to be wise, became fools; who, because when they knew God they glorified him not as God, became vain in their imagination, and their foolish heart was darkened? Did the lustre of her genius, did the liberality of her institutions, did the glorious roll of her eloquence, did the lyric sweetness of her song, save Greece from the infamy of her obliteration, when she perished under the eating cancer of her favorite sins? Did the iron sceptre or the invincible sword, did the dignity of her government or the strength of her determination, deliver Rome from the long agony of her vile corruption and pitiable decay? The fifteenth and the eighteenth centuries, for all their reviving knowledge and glittering refinement, were they not full of wickedness, covetousness, maliciousness; full of envy, murder, debate, deceit, malignity? Did not the one honor Aretino as a poet, and Poggio as a wit; and the other accept Chesterfield as a moralist, and elevated Voltaire into a sage? Yes,—and it is a lesson of which this century too has need,—knowledge without wisdom is, as even a corrupt and worldly poet has expressed it,

> "Dim as the borrowed beams of moon or stars
> To lonely, weary, wandering travellers;
> And as their twinkling tapers disappear
> When day's bright lord ascends the hemisphere,
> So pale grows Reason at Religion's sight,
> So dies and so dissolves in supernatural light."

Wisdom then is the principal thing, therefore get wisdom. But what is wisdom? The world gives the name to many higher and lower manifestations of intellectual foresight and practical sense, but Scripture sees in it nothing save one single law of life. In that most magnificent outburst of life. In that most magnificent outburst of Semitic poetry, the 28th chapter of the book of Job,—after pointing out that there is such a thing as a high and noble natural knowledge, that there is a vein for the silver, and ore of gold, and a place of sapphires, and reservoirs of subterranean fire,— the Patriarch asks, "But where shall wisdom be found, and where is the place of understanding?"— and after showing with marvellous power that it is beyond man's unaided search,—that the Depths and the Sea say "It is not in me," and Destruction and

Death have but heard the fame thereof with their ears,—then he adds, as with one great thunder-crash of concluding music, " God *understandeth the way thereof, and He knoweth the place thereof* ..... *And unto man He said, Behold, the fear of the Lord, that is wisdom ; and to depart from evil is understanding.*" And again, " The fear of the Lord is the beginning of wisdom." And again, he who, in the book of Ecclesiastes, rises step by step out of the dreary cynicism of the sated worldling into the calm confidence of a godly hope, states as the conclusion no less than as the commencement of the whole matter, " Fear God and keep His commandments, for this is the whole duty of man :" and in the Epistle of St. James, after the question, " Who is a wise man, and endued with knowledge among you ?" the answer is, not he who understandeth all mysteries, not he who can speak with the tongue of men or of angels, but " Let him show out of a good conversation his works with meekness of wisdom."

But, if this be so, perhaps some one may say, Is any knowledge worth the attainment, save the one knowledge which is wisdom ? If knowledge be full of difficulties,—if, without charity, it puffeth up,—

if he who increaseth it increaseth sorrow, why then do we labor for it with such sore travail? We toil and toil, and perhaps in a moment we fall ill, and in one day the flames of a fever calcine for ever the tablets of the earthly memory, or in one moment death comes upon us, and under its cold *"hic jacet"* buries all that we have won. Or death comes to another who has not labored, and, as that impenetrable curtain is drawn aside, there is revealed to him as by a single lightning-flash, secrets deeper ten thousand-fold than those which we have wearied ourselves in the very fire to win. Why strive then after that which death may in a moment obliterate, or disease destroy? Were it not better done as others use—not indeed to waste life in indolent frivolity or shameful sloth, but to give it all to prayer and penitence, to religious musings or charitable works? "Oh happy school of Christ," wrote Peter of the Cells to a young disciple who had complained of the weary seductions and splendid vices of the mediæval Paris,—"Oh happy school of Christ, where He teaches our heart with the word of power; where the book is not purchased nor the master paid. There, life availeth more than learning, and simplicity than science. There, none are refuted, save those who are for ever rejected, and one word of final judgment, '*Ite*' or '*Venite*,' decides all questions and all cavils for ever." It was a natural exclamation, but the answer to it is, that to the true Christian *every* school will be a school of Christ. On the ample leaf of knowledge, whether it be rich with the secrets of nature or with the spoils of time, he will read no name save the name of GOD. The great stone pages of the world will have it carved upon them legibly, as on the granite tables of Sinai, and stars will sing of it in their courses, and winds blow and waters roll. Each Science, each History, each Literature, will be to him but a fresh volume of divine revelation. We were not meant to leave those volumes clasped, or to suffer the book of life to drop out of our idle hands unread. Rather would we exclaim to each young student, as did the wise and holy St. Edmund of Canterbury, "Work as though you would live for ever; live as though you would die to day." To seek for knowledge where it is possible is the clear duty of man; to win it is the gift of God. Knowledge *apart* from wisdom is like a vestibule dissevered from its temple; but it *may* on the other hand be the worthy vestibule of that sacred shrine.

"*Felix ille,*" says St. Augustine, "*qui hæc omnia nesciat, te autem sciat;*" aye, but happier he in whom knowledge is but a spark kindled from the fountain of all heat, a sunbeam whereby he may climb to the Father of Lights. If in any soul there be, by the grace of God, health and happiness, truth and justice, purity and peace, then for that soul undoubtedly will industry be a fresh virtue, and knowledge an added grace. Knowledge is a vain thing only when it is sought out of unworthy motives and applied to selfish ends; but it becomes noble and glorious when it is desired solely for man's benefit, and consecrated wholly to God's praise. "There are some," writes St. Bernard, "who desire to know with the sole purpose that they *may* know, and it is base curiosity; and some who desire to know that they may be known, and it is base ambition; and some who desire to know that they may sell their knowledge for wealth and honor, and it is base avarice: but there are some also who desire to know, that they may be edified, and it is prudence; and some who desire to know that they may edify others, and it is charity." "My child," said St. Columban to Luanus, when he saw how ardently he devoted himself to learning, "thou hast asked a perilous gift of God. Many out of undue love of knowledge have made shipwreck of their souls." "My father," replied the boy with deep humility, "if I learn to know God, I shall never offend Him, for they only offend Him who know Him not." "Go my son," replied the Abbot, charmed with his reply; "remain firm in that faith, and the true science shall conduct thee on the road to heaven."

And therefore we earnestly ask your support to-day, a support, which as you may know, is urgently required, for this seat of sound learning as well as of religious education,—for a place where the youth of England may be trained, as have been the noblest of their fathers before them, to be not only "profitable members of the Church and Commonwealth," but also to be "hereafter partakers of the immortal glories of the Resurrection." It was, as you are aware, the avowed design of King's College that its *alumni* should be taught holily as well as wisely, and should be definitely brought up not only as scholars but as Christians. Well we know how heavy are the assaults which in these days the religion of Christ must undergo; and amid those assaults we need all the knowledge that we can. If, as men say, that religion is doomed to perish, we smile indeed in the certainty of faith, knowing that Christ has built His Church upon a rock, and that never shall the gates of Hell prevail against it; but we are ready to exclaim with the ancient hero when his battle-brunt was checked in the darkness, Ἐν δὲ φάει καὶ ὄλεσσον! Our enemies charge us with timidity and obscurantism; let us in answer, as children of the light, advance fearlessly into the battle. As far as the farthest have pressed into science, we would press; as high as the highest have soared into speculation, we would soar; as deep as the deepest have dug in search for truth, we too would dig. We are false descendants of the Crusaders if we yield to cowardice; false heirs of the Martyrs if we shrink from pain; false children and false successors of the Fathers and the Schoolmen and the Reformers if we scowl on intellect or sneer at knowledge; false to every tradition of our faith and of our history, of our vocation and of our name, if, being partakers of the divine nature, and having escaped the corruption that is in the world through lust, we do not "give all diligence to add to our faith Virtue, and to our virtue Knowledge."

And it seems to me, my brethren, that in every

word which I have spoken, I have been but feebly endeavoring to interpret and illustrate the reasons for which this college exists, namely, so far as may be, to make knowledge the handmaid of Religion, and each step in its acquisition a step also in holiness of living and certitude of faith. And therefore, in one of its departments, where its students learn to apply for the service of man the Laws of Nature, it would impress upon them that those majestic agencies, which it is given to man only to control and modify but not to change, are no mere blind passionless elemental Forces, but the creation and expression of a loving and a living Will.—And in another of its great departments, devoted to the Arts of Healing, it would teach them not only to deal tenderly with this "harp of a thousand strings," because of its delicate and beautiful organization, but, far rather, to regard each sufferer who may rely upon their skill as one for whom Christ died, and each human body as a temple—ay, even in its worst ruins, still as a temple of the living God. Who shall overrate the value of such teachings? There have been those

> "Who, in the dark dissolving human heart
> And hallowed secrets of this microcosm,

Dabbling, with shameless jest, a shameful hand
Encarnalized their spirits;"

There have been those who have marred a scientific eminence by a godless materialism; there have been those who have desecrated a noble study by a brutal irreverence:—but *here* the young student may be taught to hallow the healing art by making it yet more and more of a resemblance to the life of Him who went about doing good, and healing those who were sick of divers diseases; and here he may learn, an' if he will, to make his high profession a blessing alike to the souls and to the bodies of those with whom he deals,—a profession eminently pure and tender and unselfish—pre-eminently Christian, and therefore in exact proportion as it is so, pre-eminently great.—How invaluable again may be a teaching avowedly religious in supplementing the deficiencies, in counteracting the dangers, of a training in Ancient Literature! how may it show that the saints, and the great men, and the civilization of Christianity, transcend the loftiest achievements of heathendom; that the truest progress of humanity has been its progress under the banner of the Cross, and that with all the natural virtues and splendid heroisms of those memorable days, they yet cannot sway the soul with one thousandth part of that thrilling and tender power which lies in that invitation, so sweet and so divine, "Come unto me, all ye that labor and are heavy laden, and I will give you rest!"

Once more and lastly, there is one department of this College which is devoted to the direct and immediate study of sacred things. If it be the object of every literary training which is truly Christian to "baptize as it were the logic and literature of Greece and Rome," and to read many books that we and all others may the better read the one, it is also deeply desirable, and desirable more than ever in an age of difficulty and doubt, that the studies of those who are to be its ministers should be immediately devoted to the doctrines, the history, and the evidences of our faith. He who has been called the last of the Romans,* saw, in his famous vision, a woman full of years but of unexhausted strength, and brilliant countenance, and glowing eyes, on the lower skirt of whose garments of exquisite workmanship was inwoven the letter Φ, and on the upper the letter Θ, with letters which seemed to rise between them like the steps of a ladder. But those

* Boethius, *De Consolatione ; ad init.*

garments were aged and neglected, and a part of them seemed to have been torn away as if by violence. To mend those rent robes, to restore them from neglect, to re-supply the torn fragments, to brighten the dimmed letters which are woven upon them, to make clear once more the connection between Philosophy and Theology, to show that Theology may be indeed the "*scientia scientiarum,*" if it be animated by enthusiasm and inspired by truth, —this is the task of those who labor in the Department of Theology. And surely all these tasks are worthy of your hearty sympathy and worthy of your generous aid! Should it blunt that sympathy or diminish that aid to be informed that this Institution, so lofty in its purposes, is expressly devoted to the support and service of the English Church? If it be Patriotism to aid our country, is it mere Sectarianism to support our Church? If it was held glorious in a Spartan of old to love the civil institutions of Sparta, is it a mere narrowness in us to love the ecclesiastical polity of England? The poet says "dear city of Cecrops;" shall we not say "dear city of God?" It is probable that days of struggle and anxiety are before us. And what in those days shall support the Church of

England? Not her pride of station—that may be humiliated; not her connection with the State—that may be abruptly severed; not her magnificent endowments—they may be rudely torn away; but this—if men shall be able to say of her, as the Spirit said unto the Angel of the Church in Thyatira, "I know thy works, and charity, and service, and faith, and thy patience, and thy works; and the last to be more than the first." One of those works, and one for which she hath mighty witnesses, has surely been the high work of a Christian education. Oh, herein may her last works be ever more than her first! And though, in these days of struggling selfishness, the virtue of Public Spirit seems in most men to be well-nigh dead, may God kindle the desire, as He has granted the ability, among some of those who hear me, to help—to help cheerfully and to help munificently—in this great work to-day.

ΤΩ ΘΕΩ ΔΟΞΑ.

VIII.

WORKING WITH OUR MIGHT.

And in every work that he began in the service of the House of God, and in the Law, and in the Commandments, to seek his God, he did it with all his heart, and prospered.—2 CHRON. xxxi. 21.*

WORK, ENERGY, SUCCESS—those are the prominent conceptions brought before us by this text, and those are the main topics of the plain and familiar thoughts I must address to you this morning. The duty of work, the necessity of energy, the certainty of success,—such are the impressions which, imperfect as must be our consideration of this subject, I would yet desire, by God's grace, to leave upon your minds. You are gathered at an English public school, that you may prepare for the work of your lives, and begin it here. Now, the work of a good man in the world is mainly threefold:—Work in the ordinary business of life; work for the good of others; work to make his own

* Preached in the Chapel of Clifton College at the Annual Commemoration, June 11, 1872.

soul worthy of its eternal inheritance ; and in each of these three tasks—which are in reality blended into one—toil and energy are the appointed conditions ; with them, by God's blessing, success is the certain reward.

And here, on the threshold, I hope that not one of you—not even the youngest boy here—is in any way repelled or disheartened by the thought that work—aye, and hard work—is, in some form or other, the law of life. There is, believe me, nothing whatever stern, or repellant, or wearisome in the thought. On the contrary, if God said "In the sweat of thy brow thou shalt eat bread," He said it in mercy to a race fallen from innocence. If He cursed the ground, He cursed it for man's sake. Even the Heathen poet could say

<blockquote>
Pater ipse colendi
Haud facilem esse viam voluit.
</blockquote>

Yes, work is the best birthright which man still retains. It is the strongest of moral tonics, the most vigorous of mental medicines. All nature shows us something analogous to this. The standing pool stagnates into pestilence ; the running stream is pure. The very earth we tread on, the very air we breathe, would be unwholesome but for the agitating forces of wind and sea. In balmy and enervating regions, where the summer of the broad belt of the world furnishes man in prodigal luxuriance with the means of life, he sinks into a despicable and nerveless lassitude; but he is at his noblest and his best in those regions where he has to wrestle with the great forces of nature for his daily bread. I trust that every one of you, I trust that every rightly trained and manly English boy of this generation, feels a right scorn for a slothful, which is always a miserable life. I trust that not one is so ignorant as to fancy that a life of toil is also necessarily a life without enjoyment. Your school-life here gives you many a golden opportunity of innocent happiness; many a spring and summer day in which the world is " wrapped round with sweet air and bathed in sunshine," and " it is a luxury to breathe the breath of life." God as little grudges you these as he grudges to the weary traveller his draught of the desert spring; and he who will work but faithfully will assuredly receive of God many a free and happy day spent under the blue sky, in which he may, as it were, draw large draughts of sunshine into his bosom, and rise for happy hours with thoughts fragrant as roses, and pure as the dew upon their leaves. The man or boy who has first thoroughly done his duty,—not with eye-service, as a man-pleaser, but with singleness of heart serving God—may afterwards enjoy to the very utmost his innocent delight;—

> The hour so spent shall live
> Not unapplauded in the book of Heaven.

Yes, my brethren, only *put duty always before pleasure*. Never invert this order; never let pleasure interfere with the times of duty; never let pleasure usurp the place of duty; never let pleasure infringe on the domain of duty. To do this is to imitate those ancient Egyptians who worshipped a fly and offered an ox in sacrifice to it. And when the higher purposes of life are thus subordinated to the lower, it is but fit and natural that the higher should wither away. When the trees of the forest deliberately chose the worthless and trailing bramble for their king, it was but a just nemesis that fire should break forth from the bramble, and devour the cedars of Lebanon. But if you take work—not amusement, not indolence, not folly—as the holy and noble law of life, it shall save you from a thousand petty annoyances, a thousand precocious egotisms, a thousand sickly day-dreams and morbid discontents. I hope that all of you will admire the spirit of that eloquent and noble knight who rode into the streets of Orleans with these words enwoven in gold upon the purple housings of his saddle, *Qui non laborat, neque manducabit,* "If any will not work, neither shall he eat." I hope that all of you will feel the grandeur of that last word, spoken at York, after a life of splendid energy, by the dying Emperor Septimius Severus to his sons—*Laboremus,* "Let us toil." Oh, let each one of you learn now, learn indelibly, learn even in your boyhood, that "to pass out of the world in the world's debt, to consume much and produce nothing, to sit down at the feast of life and to go away without paying the reckoning," to have struck no blow for God, to have done no service to the cause of righteousness, is discreditable indeed even to a man ordinarily high-minded, but is to a Christian guilty and shameful; nay, is to a true Christian even impossible. The only motto for him is, "Whatsoever thy hand findeth to do, do it with thy might." The only true description of his life is, "Not slothful in business, fervent in spirit, serving the Lord."

1. Now, let us take this text first, and test it by your most ordinary life—your work here. You know that your main external work here is to profit by the studies of the place : to train yourselves by patience, attention, thought, knowledge, for any position to which in future life God may call you. Well, I am not in the least afraid to say that in this, as in all else, not only is work a duty, and energy a necessity, but also that, *with* these, success is a certainty. Of work being a duty I will say no more, because, short as is the history of your school, it proves how well you have learnt that noble lesson. I know that idleness is not a besetting temptation of this school, and that manly diligence is common among you, and, therefore, as a school you have brilliantly succeeded. And yet, perhaps, there may be some boys among you who think, with a sense of discouragement, that they, individually, have failed. Now, remember that by success in the highest sense, we do not mean gaining brilliant honors, or reaching distinguished attainments. They *can* be but for the few. But God is " no respecter of persons ;" He loves all of us, His children, and wills that in the best sense we should all succeed ; nor are the petty differences between intellect and intellect any-

thing at all to His infinitude. He who has but received the two, aye, or even the one talent, may do as good service to God, may be infinitely dearer and nobler in His sight than he who has received the ten, and may hear, no less surely than the other, that high sentence of glorious approval, " Servant of God, well done!" And when a boy who has, or thinks he has, always done his duty,—who has, or thinks he has been always diligent,—does not get on, lingers at the bottom of his form, wins no prize, makes no appreciable progress, gets superannuated, and so on,—where does the failure lie? If not in a want of diligence, then mainly, I think, in a want of energy. To get on in this sense, a boy— and especially a boy not naturally gifted—needs *energy;* he needs resolve; he needs purpose; he needs heart; he needs hope; he needs enthusiasm; he needs courage; he needs undaunted perseverance; he needs the power to say,—aye, and to mean it— *I will.* In the regions of that which is at all possible there are hardly any known limits to that which the human will can do. If a boy succeeds in nothing, is poor in work and poor in games, lets slip all his opportunities one after another, — depend upon it this is because his resolutions have been feeble, and his purposes flaccid, and his habits listless, and his will infirm; because, in a word, there has been no iron in him, but only wood and straw. Let him pray and labor, let him believe and hope and then he *cannot* fail. The great contemporary statesman gave the secret of Sir Walter Raleigh's marvellous achievements, when he said, "I know that he can toil terribly."—That is *one* side of the matter: humble and faithful dependence on the help of God is *another;* and, therefore, when St. Bonaventura, the Seraphic doctor, was asked the secret of his amazing knowledge, he pointed in silence to the crucifix, which was the only object that adorned his cell. *Ora et labora,* said grand old Martin Luther. "Prayer and painstaking," said Elliot, the lion-hearted missionary, "will accomplish everything;" nor, if he have really made trial of this, will I ever believe that any boy, in this or in any school, has cause to say that he has failed.

> So nigh is grandeur to our dust,
> So near is God to Man,
> When Duty whispers, low, "*Thou must,*"
> The youth replies "*I can.*"

2. But, secondly, while you work, you must

remember that you are not, or ought not, to be working for yourselves, or your own selfish interests alone, but also, and mainly, for the good of others. If all the law be summed up in those two commandments, " Thou shalt love the Lord God with all thy heart," and "Thou shalt love thy neighbor as thyself," then, assuredly, that work for others should begin here and now. We are not alone in this world. In communities like these it is emphatically true that no man liveth, no man dieth to himself. The lowest, dullest, youngest boy here, does, and must, and cannot help, in some way, and to some degree, influencing others. Not more surely does every word you speak make a tremulous ripple on the surrounding air, than it makes a ripple in the hearts of those around: but with this difference, that, whereas the pulse of articulated air seems soon to die away, on the other hand—

> *Our* echoes roll from soul to soul,
> And live for ever and for ever.

How vast is the power of a good boy for good, how rapid is the influence of a bad boy for evil, is a daily and deepening as well as a very solemn experience. Often in a school, or in a house, have I seen a good boy make virtue fearless and confident, and vice timid and ashamed. Often have I known boys by whose mere presence, by whose countenance, as was said of the Roman Cato, the good were inspired and the wicked checked. Often, too, have I noticed the reverse. Just as you may have seen a river bright and "pure as the tears of morning," and pellucid to its very depths, until it reaches some one spot, and there, receiving some dark admixture, its waters are stained, and the herbage withers on its banks, and, as wave after wave catches the local taint, the whole flowing river is thenceforth polluted and perturbed, and any beauty it has left is but the iridescent film over the corruption underneath,—even so it often is in the house or school. And yet in *this* case also—in the endeavor to raise the tone of those around you, in the aim to make your school, your house, your form, your dormitory, your chosen friends better than you found them,—I say again that as work is a duty, and energy a necessity, so success is a certainty. Let me show you that it is so, not by an argument, but by an instance—one instance where history might furnish hundreds—of whole communities, even in their worst condition, cleansed and ennobled by one man's influence for good. At a time when society was corrupt and hollow to its heart's core, there was one—his name was Armand de Rancè—who lived in that glittering world with immense applause. Rich, noble, eloquent, handsome, he drank the cup of pleasure to the dregs, and by God's grace, while yet young, found it unutterably bitter. For a time he fell into despair; everything seemed to fall to dust in his hand, to slip into ashes at his touch. But he was not one who, as it were, longed only to purchase a cheap forgiveness, and then still to clutch at every not absolutely forbidden comfort. No; having sinned and suffered, and been forgiven, he felt that henceforth his life was consecrated, not to easy pietisms, but to heroic endeavors. He shook off everything— wealth, love, home, fame—and retired to a monastery deep among the gloomy mountain-woods, where, as you approach, you pass by three pillars of iron, and on the first of these is engraved the word *Charity*, and on the second *Brotherly Union*, and on the third *Silence*. To this monastery he retired, and found it in a condition truly frightful. The few monks left in it were corrupt, degraded, and ignorant to the last degree. Among these he went alone, but with the avowed hope, the avowed purpose, of reforming them;—unarmed, save by the force of God, and that strong-sided champion, Conscience. Many attempts were made to waylay and murder him; one monk tried to shoot him in open day. But De Rancè never flinched. He worked with his might, and, God helping him, he prospered. His most violent persecutors became his most steadfast friends. The monk who shot at him became a most humble and holy penitent. And thus, in the irresistible might of a firm purpose and a holy courage, did one man triumph over his own enemies and the enemies of God. He came to a den of robbers and left it a house of prayer. You are not in a corrupt and dangerous place like that, but in a Christian and an English school, where thousands of good influences are at work around you; and yet, is there nothing that you can do? Are there no evils to check? No sins to conquer? No characters to be amended? No wrong-doings to be repressed?—Oh, assuredly, there is not one of you who might not make those about him better; not one of you who will not succeed in doing so if only he will faithfully try; not one who, in trying, would not win God's richest blessing on his own heart and his own life.

3. But how, my brethren, is this work possible,

how is any other work worth doing, until the initial work, the work of self-conquest, the work of setting our own hearts right with God has been performed? He who would help others to be better, must first be good himself; he who would point others to the path which leads to their Saviour's feet, must first have found it for himself. But how find it? Can it come to him in a dream? Can he stumble on it by an accident? Can he yawn it into being by a wish? Or, does it not lie rather through a strait gate? and must not *he* struggle and agonize who would pass there-through? I think that we are all liable to the danger of viewing with a fatal and paralyzing indifference our relation to God's majestic law. For though it is not difficult for any one to walk in God's ways, who, from childhood upwards, has lived in the light of his earliest prayers,—with how few, alas, is this the case! How few of us are unwounded? How many of us must sadly say "The crown is fallen from our heads, for we have sinned?" Innocence of heart, my brethren, blamelessness of life, a conscience void of offence towards God and towards man,—these are easier not to lose than when once lost to recover; and it is a fatal thing, a fatally perilous arrogance and disbelief, to be living in sin yet not in sorrow; in rebellion against God's law, yet without either penitence or fear. In this respect, therefore, pre-eminently, work is a duty; the work of conscious, steady, self-improvement: the will, nay, the resolve; nay, the solemn vow; nay, the inflexible absorbing purpose, that each year shall see us better, holier, wiser than the last. And this work, too, must be with our might; it must be in penitence, and watchfulness, and self-denial. But *then* it must and will succeed; aye, succeed with that highest of all successes,—that success which includes and exceeds all others, and beside which all others shrink into insignificance,—the prosperity of a heart at peace with God. Other prosperity may or may not follow: it generally does, but it is no great matter whether it does or not, and when it does not, that loss is more than compensated by a peace of mind which does not even desire it. No true work since the world began was ever wasted; no true life since the world began has ever failed. Oh, understand, my brethren, those two perverted words, failure and success, and measure them by the eternal not by the earthly standard. What the world has regarded as the bitterest failure has often been in the sight of

Heaven the most magnificent success. When the cap, painted with devils, was placed on the brows of John Huss, and he sank dying amid the embers of the flame,—was that a failure? When St. Francis Xavier died cold and lonely on the bleak and desolate shore of a heathen land,—was that a failure? When the frail worn body of the Apostle of the Gentiles was dragged by a hook from the arena, and the white sand scattered over the crimson lifeblood of the victim whom the dense amphitheatre despised as some obscure and nameless Jew,—was that a failure? And when, after thirty obscure, toilsome, unrecorded years in the shop of the village carpenter, One came forth to be pre-eminently the Man of Sorrows, to wander from city to city in homeless labors, and to expire in lonely agony upon the shameful cross,—was that a failure? Nay, my brethren, it was the life, it was the death, of Him who lived that we might follow in his steps—it was the life, it was the death, of the Son of God.

Oh, may you learn this lesson here and now, in this Christian chapel, the Holy of Holies of a Christian school, which, like every Christian school, is and must be a Temple of the living God! You may learn here many and valuable lessons ; but the day may come when all others shall be as dust, and the lessons learnt in this chapel be as pearls and gold. " Believe me," said an eminent man, speaking to a school like this, " believe one who tells you, from his own recollection, that if there be any time or place in which he may seem to have met the angels of God on his pilgrimage through life, it was in the midst of a congregation and in the walls of a chapel such as this. Years have rolled away, yet that chapel, with its joyful and mournful recollection, still remains a distinct and blessed spot in the memory of the past. The words which were there heard return again and again with the freshness and vividness of yesterday, to cheer and enliven, to console and solemnize, the labor and the leisure, the joys and the sorrows, not of one only who listened to them, but of many far and near, who will remember those hours and that scene as long as life and memory last. What has once been may, in its measure, be yet again."* May God grant it, and so may this School, which He has already so richly blessed, train up many and many a youthful son who shall be a

* "This is God's Host !"—A Sermon preached in Marlborough College Chapel, by the Very Rev. the Dean of Westminster.

profitable member of the Church and Commonwealth; and not this only, but—which shall be a yet more blessed and enduring crown,—many and many who, working with their might, shall, whether they prosper on earth or not, be partakers hereafter of the immortal glory of the Resurrection.

IX.

PHARISEES AND PUBLICANS.

And he spake this parable unto certain that trusted in themselves that they were righteous, and despised others.—LUKE xvii. 9.*

THE parable which our Lord spoke on this occasion told how two men went up to the Temple to pray, a Pharisee and a Publican, and while the one made his prayer a self-complacent catalogue of his own virtues, the other would not so much as lift up his eyes to heaven, but smote upon his breast, saying, God be merciful to me a sinner; and this man went down to his house justified rather than the other. You will see therefore at once that the lesson thus addressed to the proud and the self-righteous is a pointed rebuke to self-righteousness and pride; and that, strange and terrible as such a lesson might appear, those who despised others were taught that their own position must be more dangerous, more alien, less pleasing to God, than that

* Preached in Westminster Abbey (Special Evening Service, May 10, 1868).

of those whom they despised. We always find this fearless directness, this immediate pertinence, in the teaching of our Lord. Straight and swift as the arrow to the mark, his words struck full into the hearts and consciences of His hearers, and if they wounded it was not the rankling wound of an enemy, but the faithful and blessed wound of a friend who stood at hand to heal. Were there hypocrites among his hearers? He tore the mask from their faces, and held up their true semblance to themselves and to the world. Were there penitents? He flung the white robe of his mercy over their offences, and told them how they might be justified and cleansed. Were there the indifferent and the insolent? the thunder whose echo rolled upon the desert winds, were less terrible than the awful warnings of His voice. They who would rightly deliver Christ's message, must herein study His example; they must address themselves to the spiritual needs of their hearers; and if into the souls of the humble and the sorrowful their words should descend as the dew of God upon the tender grass, on the other hand to the hardened, and the scornful, and the dead in heart, that word must be a sword to pierce, a fire to calcine into dust, a hammer to dash in pieces the flinty heart. Woe to the Church which answers her worshippers according to their idols; which sinks her voice into the dull conventional murmurs of "peace, peace, when there is no peace;" which reflects too faithfully the easy and polished optimism of the world to utter aloud in all their dread significance the plain stern messages of God. If we would learn what and how to speak, we must go back to read, with no filmed vision, with no biassed perception, with no glozing heart, the clear, unmistakable words of Christ;— remembering only that He spake out of His divine and spotless innocence, and we speak but as sinful among the sinful, as weak and dying among weak and dying men.

There were, as you know, two classes to which our Lord's teachings were constantly addressed; on the one hand to Scribes and Pharisees, on the other hand to Publicans and sinners. Now mark what a rift of difference separated these two classes. The Pharisees were the well-to-do, the instructed, the religious classes, they were called Rabbi; they were honored in the synagogues; their profession of sanctity was open and ostentatious; it was worn like the phylactery upon their foreheads, and like the riband of legal blue which they made so broad upon the fringes of their robes. On the other hand the Publicans and sinners were the dregs of mankind,—the offscouring and outcasts of the people, the fallen, the friendless, the dangerous, and the despised. Their very livelihood was guilt, their name was infamy. A Pharisee regarded their mere presence as contamination, and would have shaken his robe had it but touched them in his walk. Yet how does our Lord deal with these two classes? For the latter we find no single word of bitter irony or crushing denunciation; awakement to the sense of guilt and the need of repentance was easier for them in whom self-deceit was impossible, nor did they need warning who were so burdened already with the world's agony and shame. But Christ alone spake to them of hope, and therefore His teaching dawned upon them like the dayspring upon the darkness. They came to him as awakened penitents, and He treated them as the lost sheep whom He came to save, the bruised reed which He would not break, the smoking flax He would not quench; and washed, and cleansed, and justified, they repaid with passionate devotion the pity which had touched their neglected and trembling souls. But for the others, for them whose dead hearts mistook their own hypocrisy for holiness, and their own ignorance for wisdom,—against them only that divine and loving voice seems to ring with scorn and indignation, and the lips that breathed the Beatitudes to the poor crowds who sat listening among the mountain-lilies, run over with scathing, withering, almost pitiless rebuke at their smooth hypocrisy, their ceremonial pedantry, their censorious orthodoxy, their intolerable pride. For them the crystal river of his tenderness becomes a stormy torrent of living fire. To the Publicans and harlots He gently said with that tone which broke into sobs over lost Jerusalem, "Come unto me, all ye that labor and are heavy laden, and I will give you rest;" but to the Scribes and Pharisees He cried in tones of doom and wrathfulness, "Ye fools and blind; blind guides, blind Pharisees; ye serpents, ye generation of vipers, how can ye escape the damnation of hell?"

Burning words, my brethren, and such as may well astonish us; men who have borrowed their morality from Christianity, and used that very morality to criticise its divine source, have ventured to condemn them. That men *have* so ventured to condemn,—that even to us, who believe in the

Lord Jesus Christ, they come with a shock of surprise as though at first sight they were inconsistent with loving and sacred tenderness—is a proof that they need our most serious attention : it is a proof surely that they belong to some aspect of his character which hitherto we have not rightly understood. And such is pre-eminently the case. Christian art, Christian eloquence, Christian song have long made us familiar with Christ's meekness and lowliness of heart ; they have portrayed him most often as the Man of Sorrows ; they have lost themselves in the infinitude of his suffering and his love. But it is ever our danger to realize but half the truth ; and there is one side of our Lord's character which, because it has not sufficiently been dwelt upon, has scarcely exercised its due influence upon our minds. It is his just indignation. The ideal of the Christian life,—not the true ideal, but the common one, —has been too tame, too timid, too effeminate ; strange as it may seem, it has wanted not only that brightness and joyance, that high victorious faith, that royalty of happiness, which of due right belong to it, but it has been lacking also in that fire and force, that iron in the blood, that dauntless courage, that glorious battle-brunt in the heart of man, which are yet necessary to soldiers of the Cross. Yes, amid the perplexed hypocrisies of civilization, amid the hollow insincerities which permeate our very forms of speech,—it seems as though we never dared that intensity of purpose, that burning moral indignation, that splendid passion of scorn and hatred against all that is corrupt and base, which lends to the words of Psalmist and Prophet their eternal significance. The old mighty, unswerving, heart of Christendom seems dead. We dare not face our thoughts; we dare not act up to our convictions; we are full of conventional phrases, and polite reticence, and soft compromise, under which is smothered that fire which of old burnt in men's hearts till at the last they spake with their tongue. There is indeed a wrath, as you read in Scripture, an ignoble wrath, which worketh not the righteousness of God; but there is also a wrath of righteous indignation, which is not permissible only, but also pre-eminently noble. Such was the wrath which nerved the strong right arm of Phinehas, when he stayed the shameful apostacy of Israel with one thrust of his avenging spear; such was the wrath wherewith Elijah bearded and smote at their own altar the priests of Baalim,—such the wrath which flames in every unrenevated heart under intense love of right and intense hate of wrong. We see it in the great forerunner, when he braved in their tyranny the bloodstained tyrant and the adulterous queen ; we see it in our blessed Lord when he overthrew the tables of the money-changers and drove them from the Temple with his knotted scourge ; we see it in him whose whole nature seems to have caught the lightnings which flashed in his face as he journeyed to Damascus ;— we see it in those great martyrs who with "the unresistible might of weakness shook the world ; "— we see it in Origen, and Athanasius, and Augustine, and Bernard, and Luther, and Knox, and Milton, and Whitfield, and Wilberforce. There was no half-heartedness of judgment, no timidity of compromise, in the thoughts and words of men like these. They spoke as their Master spoke, and if ever a worldly age is to be startled from its torpor, it must be by voices like to theirs. Such men may be stigmatized, as hot and rude, and violent, but oh! better is the clearing hurricane than the brooding pestilence ; better their sacred fury than the sleepy selfishness of a smooth prosperity : better, as has been truly and boldly said, better are agonies of pain and blood shed in rivers than souls spotted and bewildered with mortal sin.

But, if from Christ's example we must learn the duty of fervency, and the necessity for righteous indignation, I know nothing which it more solemnly imports us to realize than the conditions which kindled that lofty passion. Is there anything in us, or in our circumstances, like that which moved the wrath of the Lamb, and made the messages of denunciation fall with such fearful emphasis from the lips of perfect love? Were the steps of our Master in this city now, are there any like those Publicans whom He so deeply pitied,—any like those Pharisees against whom he uttered so terrible an anger, though He well knew that He was thus awakening the resentment which would nail Him at last to the bitter cross?

Ah, my brethren, the first at any rate of these classes is never far to seek. Will you find them in this fair Cathedral? No! they are not here. In God's sight indeed,—to those eyes infinitely brighter than the sun, which pierce into the naked human heart,—there may have been some whose prayers this evening have been but "a noise of men and women between dead walls," and there may be some criminal among those here present, whose crime were it known would even make him amenable to the broken laws of man. But if there be any such, —and we know that ere now such have knelt in the sanctuary among God's Saints,—yet it is not of such criminals that congregations are composed. Happy might it be for us if we could gather more of them into our Churches;—happy if we could make them feel that they, even they, in their sinfulness and shame, belong indeed to the Church's fold; —happy if we could seek them as the shepherd seeks his lost and wandering sheep;—happy if we could teach them to believe that the joy of the Church on earth over one sinner that repenteth, is the same in kind as that which causes a fresh strain of exultation to ring from the harps of heaven. So far as we can do this, are we doing the work that Christ loves best. For His soul yearned towards them,—nor was there any lesson that He better loved to teach than the lesson that they too might still repent and return and be received with love in the home from which they had wandered;—that in spite of all their errors and all their crimes they were still dear to that heavenly Father who is full of tenderness to all His children,—who maketh His sun to shine upon the evil and on the good, and His rain to fall on the just and on the unjust.

But if the criminal classes—the Publican and the sinner—exist no less in modern England than in ancient Palestine, and if we, here assembled, assuredly do not belong to the number of open, flagrant, and defiant sinners, is there on the other hand no resemblance in us, inwardly no less than outwardly, to those well-to-do, respectable, religious classes, who stood so fair in the world's eye, but whom He who was the Truth, and who came to reveal God to man, compared to whited sepulchres full of dead men's bones,—to graves which appear not, so that they who walk over them are not aware of them? Are there among us no full-fed Sadducees, who believe neither in angel nor spirit;—no temporizing Herodians anxious only for quiet and success;—no orthodox Scribes fiercely eager about the letter of the law, profoundly ignorant of its spirit;—none like those worldly Priests and violent Pharisees, who, in the desperate blindness of the human heart, persuaded themselves doubtless that they were the friends of God, while they were arraying every engine of popular ignorance, and established power, against His image in His Son? The form indeed is changed, but must we not ask ourselves with deep humility whether the spirit may not still remain? We too are not extortioners, unjust, adulterers, or even as these publicans; yet can it be that some of us also may be the children of wrath, even as others, —can it be that of us also there are some whose dull and selfish lives are so displeasing to God, that they shall stand hereafter in the full front of His displeasure, and hear from a Father most loving, from a Judge most merciful, that chilling, crushing, heart-appalling sentence, "I never knew you; depart from me, ye workers of iniquity."

I for one, my brethren, cannot approach this question with the easy confidence of our smooth popular theology; I cannot profess to approach it without deep and anxious misgiving; I cannot clearly see in what respect we are exempt from danger lest our religion should not exceed the religion of the Scribes and Pharisees. Certainly when we look round us on the world of ordinary respectability it looks fair enough. Yet it takes no very keen observation to note many and unlovely stains on the white surface of our conventionality. Strip the iridescence from the surface of the standing pool, and the stagnant waters putrefy below. Under that glittering film of surface-respectability lie evils which, as has been well said, "vex less, but mortify more, which suck the blood though they do not shed it, and ossify the heart though they do not torture it." That the age in which we live is full of restlessness and discontent,—that it is an age but half sincere in its beliefs,—that it is sinking more and more deeply into luxury and self-indulgence,— that it is agitated with an emulous and feverish desire for wealth,—that it is afflicted with a deep unchristian sadness and anxiety,—we learn not so much from our preachers as from our daily moralists. It is an age not of great crime, but of little meannesses; there are few murders, but plenty of malice; little blasphemy, but universal cynicism; rare open thefts, but widespread secret dishonesty. And the worst sign is that the Church has well-nigh ceased to be fruitful of pre-eminent saintliness; few lights shine out distinctly from the general darkness. Good and evil seem to be at truce, "lying together flat upon the world's surface. Our very conception of goodness seems to be dwarfed and impoverished; and so little do we attain the high and heroic ideal of the Gospel, that men have begun to argue openly that it is an ideal which is in these days obsolete and impossible. Little, alas! do we act up to our high profession, and we know to our deep shame that the world has some ground for its bitter taunt, that often men who call themselves children of the kingdom are as ready to take offence, and as prompt to repeat calumny, and as hard to drive a bargain, and as eager for gain, and as anxious for power, and as bitter and as contemptuous to those who differ from them in matters of opinion, as though they were not professed disciples of Him who was a village carpenter,—of Him who prayed for His murderers, —of Him who shrank not from the white leper's loathly touch, and felt no horror when the tears of the forgiven harlot flowed fast on His unsandalled feet.

But since it is fatally easy to see the faults of others, let us look rather at our own hearts. And, though most of us may be wholly free from open and notorious sins, our conception of our high calling in Christ Jesus must be mean indeed, if that suffice. So were the Pharisees who crucified their Lord. Fear, happy circumstances, the absence of temptation,—nay, even prudential calculation,—may save a man from sinning thus; and yet the publicans and harlots may go into the kingdom of

God before him. Our lives may be correct before men ; but God seeth the heart ; and our hearts, are they right with God ? Is the glory of the Spirit indeed bright within those spiritual temples, or is there many an unhallowed idol in their inmost chambers ? The real danger and ruin of guilt rests not so much in the poison which it infuses into society, not so much in its deadly and fatal consequences to the well-being of nations, not so much in any outward circumstances of punishment and retribution, as in that alienation of the soul from God, that gradual, slow-creeping mystery of spiritual death of which men are often themselves unconscious, until God suffers them,—as he suffered David,—t(fall into some great·sin, which lights up the theati of the soul with a glare of unnatural illumination, and reveals to them the true horror of themselves. Out of the heart proceed evil thoughts ;—evil thoughts, and then, as though thereby the floodgates of iniquity were opened,—murders, adulteries, and all the black and terrible sins whose catalogue you know. When the Scribes and Pharisees dragged into Christ's sacred presence a sinful and fallen woman, and He said, " Let him that is without sin among you cast the first stone at her,"—is there not a solemn warning to us in the fact that those words pierced the thick self-deception of dead consciences, and one by one,—without even His eye upon them to make the blush burn upon the guilty cheek,—one by one, self-convicted, self-condemned, —one by one, white-robed priest, and scrupulous Pharisee, and self-complacent scribe,—one by one, boy, and maiden, and old man, beginning from the eldest unto the last,—abased by the sudden recognition of their own inward guilt, they rose and stole from the Temple precincts, and left none there save the Redeemer and the redeemed? Oh! would it not be so with us if Christ were here? and He *is* here; and though now we see Him not, one day we shall stand before his Holy eye ; and the moral sensibility must be very dead in that man, who, in the filthy rags of his own righteousness, could meet that gaze before which the very heavens are not clean. Oh, let us not deceive ourselves: this contented acquiescence in ignoble efforts, this lukewarm subservience to a low and unworthy standard, is the peculiar disease of this century, and the peculiar danger of a soft, luxurious, unvexed career. Alas! the primrose path may lead only to the edge of the precipice ; and even if our lives be externally free from every grave offence against the law of God, can we afford to obliterate wholly from our memories those two parables of Christ about the two men,—wealthy, successful, respected, free from crime,—yet for one of whom there was only that thundercrash of judgment, " Thou fool, this night," and the silence which followed it;—and for the other only that lurid picture—aye, it may well appal us, yet Christ drew it —that lurid picture of one carried from purple, and fine linen, and sumptuous feast, to the burning thirst and the tormenting flame?

And when I think of these things, my brethren, I feel, as I said before, a deep misgiving,—a misgiving which I cannot gloss over or disguise,—lest some of us be guiltier even than the openly guilty, and lest with more than the blessings of Chorazin and Bethsaida we suffer more than the condemnation of Sidon and of Tyre. Without life in the spirit,—without the fire of God's love burning bright on the altar of the regenerated heart,—how can we enter into the kingdom of God? And the dull comforts of the world,—the blind, groping, illiberal absorption in some mechanical routine,—the earthliness of a life toiling for riches, clogged with cares, surfeited with indulgence,—these are the things which, if we be not very humble and very careful, more than all others quench the spiritual perception, and, in the scornful concentration of the Psalmist's language, make the heart grow *fat as brawn*. It is not a Christian minister, it is a secular historian who says that of all unsuccessful men, in every shape, "whether divine or human, there is none equal to Bunyan's Facing-both-ways,—the fellow with one eye on heaven and one on earth,—who sincerely preaches one thing and sincerely does another, and from the intensity of his unreality is unable even to see or feel the contradiction. He is substantially trying to cheat both God and the devil, and is in reality only cheating himself and his neighbor. This of all characters upon the earth appears to me to be the one of which there is no hope at all,—a character becoming in these days alarmingly abundant." Do we not find a significant commentary on these words in the blank surprise of John the Baptist, when Scribes and Pharisees came to his ministry—"O generation of vipers, who hath warned *you* to flee from the wrath to come?" The robber and the Publican, the ignorant peasant and the brutal soldier—it is natural that these should come: but what has the wild rude prophet

of the desert and his doctrine of repentance to do
with you, and your dead sanctities, and your despicable orthodoxies, and your "Stand aside, for I
am holier than thou?" Aye, it might well seem
impossible that anything should arouse respectable
men whose consciences have fallen into a death-like
slumber, as they slave at their farm and their merchandise, and think that they have successfully
solved the problem of serving alike their Mammon
and their God. There are some men whose sins are
open, going before to judgment, marshalling them
with pointed finger and tumultuous condemnation,
haling them with open violence and public shame
before the bar : but, when our sins are only following
after us unseen, with stealthy footsteps and invisible
array, when the long accumulations of malice and
meanness, and avarice, and impurity—when the
false and settled habits of a worldly and selfish re-
ligionism gather in our rear in ever-increasing
multitudes, ready to crowd upon the stricken memory when death lets in upon the self-deceiving soul
the chill light of eternity,—then our condition,
though less molested and less notorious, may be
more full of peril. Oh, better by far that God
should break us with His indignation, and vex us

with all His storms,—better that He should make us suffer in every fibre of our being the ignoble martyrdom of sin,—better that His lightnings should shatter the lowest bases of our earth-born happiness, and let the nether fires glare in our very faces, than that He should thus suffer our souls, under this terrible danger of His wrath, to slumber on, in this trance of despairing insensibility, in this unconsciousness of commencing death.

For, believing that God's wrath against sin is established in inexorable laws,—believing that He has revealed that wrath as plainly as if He had engraved it upon the sun, or written it in stars upon the midnight sky,—then casting my thoughts beyond death, and fixing them seriously there, my heart shivers like a leaf in some cold wind ; and an earnest, hearty, entire repentance, a searching, honest, unshrinking self-examination, appear to be the very work of life. Oh, we have all need of that prayer of the Breton mariner, " Save us, O God, thine ocean is so large, and our little boats so small." Smoothly indeed now,—like some frail vessel, with white sail and streaming pennon, we may be gliding over the calm and sunlit waves, yet without God's love we may find at last that this dead sea of life was but a sea of glass mingled with fire,—a sea in which no haven opens, nor any light-house shines, —a sea whose depths are unfathomable and whose rolling waters have no shore. Ah, if our ship founder in that sea, it will be too late to know things in their true light, too late to be alarmed. Like those of whom our Saviour so sadly spoke,—and oh! my brethren, consider for ourselves if the picture be not as terrible as it is true,—we too may pass away from our weeping families, from our mourning friends; we may leave the white marble to record our blameless lives; we may have got the money or the success for the sake of which we forgot God, and, passing into His presence, we may expect to be received at His marriage-feast. And coming then before His great white Throne with the familiar words "Lord, Lord" upon our lips, we shall plead our diligence and our usefulness, our amiable characters, our decent professions, our moral lives, but, even while our tongues falter with fear and misgiving, the numberless phantoms of forgotten but recorded and unrepented sins, from childhood to youth, from youth to manhood, from manhood to old age, shall be thronging like thick clouds between us and our Judge;—and, like the tolling of some bell of death, shall fall, stroke after stroke, upon our ears the judgments of Scripture, " Ye cannot serve God and Mammon ; " " Ye did it not unto these little ones ; " " He that offendeth in one point is guilty of all ; " " He that trusteth in his own heart is a fool ; " —and then, at last, in a voice which mingles the awfulness of death, judgment, and eternity, " Cast out the unprofitable servant."

Oh, to no one of us may this ever be ! I have not spoken, God forbid ! to make those hearts sad which God has not made sad, but I have spoken these words of warning, my brethren, because in this life we have all need of frequent warning—because I have supposed them to be needed by others, knowing them to be needed by myself. And let us remember that the lessons of God's wrath against sin are in reality the lessons of His love for a sinful race. God shews His love by destroying that in us which would keep us from Him. He would save us, even by fire, from that spiritual death which, unawakened, ends in eternal death. And he will save us if we seek Him. While life lasts there is possible for every one of us an eternal and glorious hope. The purple thunderclouds which gather around a sinful path, may dim, indeed, but they cannot wholly obliterate the rainbow which spans their gloom. I look on this great congregation, and I say, in God's name, that there is not one immortal being among you all for whose soul the great Father who made it does not yearn; not one whom He does not long to reckon in the days that He maketh up His jewels; not one, however soiled with sinful stains, for whom Christ did not die. And therefore the grace of God still calleth you to repentance. If we perish, we perish wilfully; but no living soul, not one of all those millions of human beings who are now breathing on the surface of the globe, *need* be cut off from the mercy and peace of God. Oh, let us then beware of hard, dead, presumptuous, worldly hearts—the insidious leaven of the Pharisees and of Herod. Let us, with God's help, work out our own salvation with fear and trembling; and that we may soon attain to that perfect love which casteth out fear, and is a nobler and better thing, let us all breathe this very night, not with the lips only, but in the deep sincerity of penitent and trembling hearts, that heaven-blessed prayer of the broken and contrite publican,

"God be merciful to me a sinner."

X.

TOO LATE.

If thou hadst known, even thou, at least in this thy day, the things which belong unto thy peace! but now they are hid from thine eyes.—LUKE xix. 42.

ON Friday evening, a week before the Crucifixion, our Lord arrived at Bethany, the sweet and quiet home of Martha and Mary and Lazarus whom He loved. On the evening of the next day,—the Jewish Sabbath,—the little family made in His honor that memorable feast, in which the love of Mary, glowing into sudden rapture, led her to break the vase of alabaster, and anele with precious spikenard her Saviour's feet. The presence of the risen Lazarus added to the scene a touch of awe. Many Jews from Jerusalem, who had strolled to the little village when the setting sun removed the Sabbath restriction of distance, mingled among the guests; and as they returned to the city, through the tents and booths of the thronging pilgrims, they

* Preached at Hereford Cathedral on Palm Sunday, 1871.

were able to answer the eagerly-debated question, whether Jesus,—in spite of the violence with which He had been treated in His last visit to Jerusalem,— would still venture to be present at the Paschal feast. Yes! the great Prophet would indeed be there!

The rumor spread more and more widely as the morning dawned; and it was apparently towards the busy noon, that, accompanied by a vast throng of Galilean pilgrims, our Lord started on foot from the friendly home under the palms of Bethany. The main road from the village to Jerusalem wound round the southern shoulder of the Mount of Olives; and when it brought Him near the fig-gardens of Bethphage, Jesus dispatched two of His disciples, to fetch for His use an ass's colt, which had never before been ridden. St. Mark, reflecting the vivid memories of St. Peter, tells us how they found it tied up to a door in the street; and when the owners willingly resigned it, the disciples, thrilling with intense excitement,—for surely now, at last, the great Messianic kingdom of their hopes was to be revealed —flung their garments over it to do regal honor to their Lord. Then they lifted Him upon it, and the triumphal procession started on its way. They had advanced but a short distance when there came, round the shoulder of the hill, another festal throng which had streamed forth to meet Him from Jerusalem, waving in the sunny air the green branches which they had torn from the neighboring palms. All were full of awful expectation. The tale of the recent raising of Lazarus was on every lip. At last, swept away by uncontrollable emotion, the disciples began to raise those passionate cries of "Hosanna to the Son of David," which formed part of the great Hallel of their festal services. A scene of intense enthusiasm ensued. Breaking into involuntary acclamations, the whole multitude,—as they pealed forth the burden of the strain,—began to fling off their talliths, and spread them on the dusty road to tapestry His path; while others kept plucking, from the roadside trees, the boughs of fig and olive to strew them on His way. And so, with ringing Hosannas and waving palms—one multitude preceding, another following, the disciples grouped around—the Saviour approached the Holy City. It was no seditious movement of political indignation;—it was no insulting vanity of self-asserting pre-eminence. It was but the triumph of the poor: it was but the lowly pomp of one who rode to die. The haughty Gentiles ridiculed the

14

very record of it; and yet, besides the tragic grandeur of its real majesty, what king's or consul's triumph has had one tithe of such power to move the heart?

At the time, however, even the disciples did not understand it, nor did they recall till afterwards the prophecy of Zechariah about "the king meek and bringing salvation, lowly and riding upon an ass." They expected something wholly different from what occurred; they still hankered for some material victory. Would He not, even now, restore the kingdom to Israel? Had not the demons discerned Him, and fled His gaze? Had not heaven recognized Him, and lit her stars? Had not earth known Him, and hushed her winds? Had not the rough sea heard Him, and stilled his waves? Why should not the humble Prophet of the poor now burst forth as the irresistible avenger of the mighty? Why should He not, even now, change the ass's colt for the chariots of God which are twenty thousand, and, amid the rushing of congregated wings, drive down in thunder upon insulting Roman and apostate priest? Had not the supreme moment come? did not the hand point to the hour on the dial-plate of heaven?

Yes! the moment had come: yes! the hand pointed to the hour,—but not as they hoped.—The road from Bethany slopes up the Mount of Olives, through green fields and shady trees, till, as it suddenly sweeps round towards the north, Jerusalem, which has hitherto been hidden, bursts full upon the view. Many a traveller has reined his horse at that memorable spot with feelings too deep for speech. But the Jerusalem of that day,—as Jesus saw it under the burning flood of vernal sunshine, wrapped in its imperial mantle of proud towers,— the Jerusalem whose massive ramparts and lordly palaces made it a wonder of the world,—was a spectacle incomparably more magnificent than the decayed and crumbling city of to-day. And as there,—through the transparent atmosphere,—towering above the deep umbrageous valleys which surrounded it,—the city reared into the morning sunlight its multitudinous splendors of marble pinnacle and golden roofs,—was there no pride, no gladness, in the heart of its true King? Far otherwise! An indescribable sorrow seized Him. He paused. The procession halted. All the tumult of acclaim was hushed. The glad cries sank into silence. And, as Jesus gazed, a rush of divine sorrow and compassion welled up from His inmost heart. He had dropped silent tears at the grave of Lazarus; here, over fallen Jerusalem, He wept aloud. Five days afterwards, all the shame of His mockery, all the anguish of His torture, were unable to extort from Him one single sob, or to wet his eyelids with one trickling tear; but now an infinitude of yearning pity and trembling love overmastered His whole spirit, and He not only wept, but burst into a passion of lamentation in which the choked voice seemed to struggle for utterance.—Strange Messianic triumph! Mournful interruption of those exultant Hosannas! As He gazed on David's Sion,—as He stood before the Jerusalem of the prophets and the kings,—the King, the Deliverer, the son of David, wept!

And why?—At His feet the olives were flinging their broad shadows over green Gethsemane, the scene of His coming agony,—but it was not that. Opposite Him, on the rocky plateau beyond the Kidron, Calvary was waiting for His cross of torture, —but it was not that. Nay, but it was something which no eye saw but His. For He was gazing, with the eagle glance of prophecy, on a scene far different from that which met his actual gaze. What He saw was, not a fair and holy city, sitting, like a lady of kingdoms, upon her virgin heights,—but a city cowering, abject, degraded, desolate. To Him the faithful city has become a harlot. Her gold has become dross; her wine mixed with water; and now her hour had come. In the Jerusalem that was—the glittering Jerusalem of the days of Herod and Tiberius—He saw, down the dim vista of fifty years, the Jerusalem that was to be,—the desecrated Jerusalem of the days of Titus. He saw those lordly towers shattered,—those umbrageous trees hewn down,—that golden sanctuary polluted,—Judæa Capta a desolate woman, weeping under her palm-tree amid her tangled hair. In the flush of the existing prosperity He foresaw the horrors of the coming retribution. The eye of His troubled imagination beheld the 600,000 corpses carried out of those city-gates ;—the wretched fugitives crucified by myriads around those walls;—the priests, swollen with hunger, leaping madly into the devouring flames, until those flames had done their purging, scathing, avenging work, and what had been Jerusalem, the holy, the noble, was but a heap of ghastly ruins where the smouldering embers were half-slaked in the rivers of a guilty nation's blood.

And as He saw it,—as this vision of the future rushed red upon His gaze,—as He recalled the promise of peace which the very name of the city breathed, and knew that she would see peace again no more,—this Saviour whom they rejected, whom they hated, whom they crucified, cried aloud in a broken voice, and with eyes that streamed with tears, "If thou hadst known, even thou, at least in this thy day, the things that belong unto thy peace,"—"If thou hadst known,"—and indeed those words seemed to summon up yet another picture,—not of Jerusalem as she *was*,—not of Jerusalem as she *was to be*,—but of Jerusalem as she *might have been*,—yes! of a Jerusalem little less glorious than her of the prophet's vision, descending out of heaven with her walls of jasper and gates of pearl,—of that Jerusalem about whom so many glowing hearts have sung,—

> Oh happy harbor of the saints,
>   Oh sweet and pleasant soil,
> In thee no sorrows may be seen,
>   No pain, no grief, no toil.
>
> Thy houses are of ivory,
>   Thy windows crystal clear,
> Thy tiles they are of beaten gold,
>   O would that I were there!

> Right through the streets, with silver sound,
> The flood of life doth flow,
> Upon whose banks, on either hand,
> The trees of life do grow.

Alas! it was all a glorious "if"—a heartrending "might have been." It was as when a traveller stands on some great misty mountain-top,—longing to gaze on the magnificent expanse of city, and plain, and river, and the rippling sea,—and for one moment, through one great rent of the enshrouding mist, he looks on a fairy vision, bathed in sunlight and overarched with iris,—but, almost before he has seen it, the rent in the mist is closed once more, and ragged and grey the clouds roll up, and he is alone, and miserable, and chill, and disenchanted. Even so was it with that momentary glimpse of the possible Jerusalem; it was, alas! but a vanishing "might have been," and

> Of all sad words of tongue and pen
> The saddest are those "It might have been."

It might have been—but it was not: it never would be now; and love, after doing all in vain, could only weep. "If thou hadst known—even thou—at least in this thy day—the things that belong unto thy peace;"—if—and there sorrow suppressed the apodosis; and when the sob, which broke His voice, was over, He could only add " but now they are hid from thine eyes."

And herein, my brethren, lies the meaning of this scene for us; this is the lesson on which I would desire to fix our hearts this evening. May I not hope, that, even now, in part at least, your hearts and consciences have been interpreting it into words? It is an awful, but it is also, for that very reason, a blessed lesson: and oh may God give me wisdom to speak, and give you hearts to realize, alike its awful and its blessed side!

1. The awful side is this. There, before the Saviour's gaze of tears, lay a city, splendid apparently and in peace, and destined to enjoy another half century of existence. And the day was a common day; the hour a common hour: no thunder was throbbing in the blue unclouded sky; no deep voices of departing deities were rolling through the golden doors: and yet,—soundless to mortal ears in the unrippled air of Eternity,—the knell of her destiny had begun to toll: and, in the voiceless dialect of heaven, the fiat of her doom had been pronounced; and in that realm which knoweth and needeth not any light save the light of God, the sun

of her moral existence had gone down while it yet was day.—Were her means of grace over? No, not yet. Was her Temple closed? No, not yet. Were her services impossible? No, not yet. The white-robed Levites still thronged her courts; the singers still made the heavens ring with their passionate litanies and silver Psalms; the High Priest yet sprinkled, year by year, the gold of the holiest altar with the blood of unavailing sacrifice. No change was visible in her to mortal eyes. And yet, for her, from this moment even until the end, the accepted time was over, the appointed crisis past,—the day of salvation had set into irrevocable night. It was with her as with the barren fig-tree, on which, next day, the Lord pronounced His doom. The leaf of her national life was still glossy-green; the sun still shone on her; the rain fell; the dew stole down; but the fruit would grow on her no more, and therefore the fire was kindled for the burning, the axe uplifted, which would crash on the encumbering trunk. She was not spared for her beauty; she was not forgiven for her fame. And if it were so with the favored city, may it not be so with thee, and thee, and me? What shall the reed of the desert do, if even the cedar be shattered at a blow?—Yes:

the lesson of the tears of Jesus over Jerusalem, as she gleamed before Him in the vernal sunshine, a gem upon her crown of hills, is this: and oh may we all have grace to learn it now—learn it even in this solemn week: that, as for her, so for us, there may be a too-late; the door may be shut without a sound; the doom sealed without a sigh; life may be over before death comes. It is not—(oh mark this!)—it is not that God loses His mercy, but that we lose our capacity for accepting it: it is not that God hath turned away from us, but that we have utterly paralyzed our own power of turning back to Him. And then the voice sighs forth with unutterable sadness, "Ephraim is turned unto idols, let him alone." Let him alone, O preacher, for he hates the words of truth! let him alone, O Word of God, for he hath set his face as a flint against thee; let him alone, O Conscience, for he is bent on murdering thee; his sins have become not wilful only but willing; he has chosen them,— let him have them. He has loved death more than life, and lies rather than righteousness, and vice more than virtue, and the world more than heaven, and the lusts of the flesh rather than the law of God. And the Spirit of God hath striven with him, and striven in vain: all, all hath been in vain: let him alone: let him eat of the fruit of his own works, and be filled with his own devices.

O fearful voice of most just judgment! and yet observe further, as a still more solemn source of warning, that, at the very instant when this dread fiat is sounding forth, we may be all unconscious of it. Jerusalem knew not—she was wholly unaware—that this was the last day of her visitation. She had quenched the light of life,—but dreamed not of the hastening midnight: she had silenced the voice of warning, and suspected not that the hush which followed was but the hush before the hurricane,—the silence before the trumpet's sound. Sick—she knew it not: dying—she knew it not. "Ephraim hath gray hairs upon him, and he knoweth it not." It is, alas! ever thus. This is the very method of God's dealings with us,—not by stupendous miracles but by quiet warnings; not by shocks of catastrophe, but by processes of law. The Holy Light is but a beam shining quietly in the darkness, easily strangled in the wilful midnight: the pleading voice is but a low whisper amid the silence, easily drowned in the tempest of the passions. And so, though the day of grace has its fixed limits, and these may be often narrower than the day of life, we neither know what those limits are, nor when they are transcended. And if ours be a guilty ignorance, a penal blindness, we *cannot* know. So that then the presumptuous sinner may be in this awful condition :—A temptation may come to him,—perhaps a temptation to some besetting sin to which he has often and often yielded, and stifling the last faint whisper of conscience he may sin once more; and after that conscience speaks no more ; and for the sake of that one last miserable sin, he has lost his soul. Or perhaps it is one last call to repentance ; and because he has rejected it so often, he carelessly and wilfully once more rejects it ; and after that, the call comes again no more for ever, and the things that belong unto his peace are hid for ever from his eyes. Life continues, but it is really death ; and on the dead soul in the living body the gates of the eternal tomb have closed.

2. Can there be a blessed side to truths so true, and yet so full of solemnity and judgment as these? Yes, if we will it, a most blessed side. Seeing that there is good in the world, and there is evil in the world, and that the evil is ruin, and misery, and death, and that the good is blessing, and hope, and

peace,—and that we can, if we will, choose the evil and reject the good and so destroy ourselves for time and for eternity,—what can God in his mercy do more merciful than to make evil terrible to us, if so be we may be averted from it? And the more terrible evil becomes to our inmost nature,—the more, out of very hatred and horror, we turn away from it as from our utmost bane, the happier are we. And therefore everything is blessed which is meant to make us tremble at sin, every doctrine, however awful, is blessed if it helps to startle us from that fatal drunkenness, to wean us from that fatal fascination. The object of all terror is persuasion: of all warning prevention: of all danger repentance. The object of all that I have said is this, "Judge therefore yourselves, brethren, that ye be not judged of the Lord." All our lives are in some sense a "might have been;" the very best of us must feel, I suppose, in sad and thoughtful moments, that he might have been transcendantly nobler, and greater, and loftier than he is: but, while life lasts, every "might have been" should lead, not to vain regrets, but to manly resolutions; it should be but the dark background to a "may be" and a "will be" yet. "Arise then, and flee to the stronghold, ye prisoners of hope."

Every one of us may be saved: every one of us may be forgiven; every one of us may be sanctified: every one of us may break even the iron fetters of besetting sins; every one of us may be brought to love so well everything that is good, and true, and pure, that we shall loathe, even in thought, the thing that is evil. As we love our souls let us strive after this end with every energy of our lives. If we are striving,—not loving our sins, but hating them,—not yielding to them, but, heart and soul, fighting against them, then God is with us and we are safe: but if, on the other hand, we have for months and years been growing colder, deader, more indifferent to God and Christ,—if we can listen now unmoved to what would once have impressed and affected us,—if we can dally now with temptations which we should once have shunned,—if we can now commit sins from which we would once have shrunk,—by these marks we may be sure that our day of grace has been declining,— that the shadows of its evening are lengthening out, —and that, if no change occur, then, "ere the sun of our natural existence has gone down, the sun of our spiritual day may have set, never to rise again." Oh, my brethren, who knows whether these very days of Passion Week may not be for us the day of our visitation? Let us all pray that they do not pass in vain? Now the door of repentance stands open, and Heaven's light streams through it ;—now in all love and gentleness the voice of our Saviour calls :—now the Holy Spirit of God still strives with us in our wanderings, still pleads for us in our failures ;—now, but who shall say how long? not for ever: not, it may be, even all our lives: not even it may be, for many days. Oh, to-day if ye will hear his voice, harden not your hearts.

XI.

PRAYER, THE ANTIDOTE TO SORROW.

And being in an agony, He prayed.—LUKE xxii. 44.*

WHEN the last supper was over, and the last hymn had been sung, our Lord and His Apostles—with the one traitor fatally absent from their number—went out of the city gate, and down the steep valley of the Kidron to the green slope of Olivet beyond it. Solemn and sad was that last walk together; and a weight of mysterious awe sank like lead upon the hearts of those few poor Galileans as in almost unbroken silence,—through the deep hush of the Oriental night,—through the dark shadows of the ancient olive-trees,—through the broken gleams of the Paschal moonlight,—they followed Him, their Lord and Master, who, with bowed head and sorrowing heart, walked before them to His willing doom.

* Preached before Her Majesty the Queen, in the private Chapel, Windsor; and, subsequently, at Marlborough College.

That night they did not return as usual to Bethany, but stopped at the little familiar garden of Gethsemane, or "the oilpress." Jesus knew that the hour of His uttermost humiliation was near,—that from this moment till the utterance of that great cry which broke His heart, nothing remained for Him on earth, save all that the human frame can tolerate of torturing pain, and all that the human soul can bear of poignant anguish;—till in that torment of body and desolation of soul, even the high and radiant serenity of His divine spirit should suffer a short but terrible eclipse. One thing alone remained before that short hour began; a short space was left Him, and in that space He had to brace His body, to nerve his soul, to calm His spirit by prayer and solitude, until all that is evil in the power of evil should wreak its worst upon His innocent and holy head. And He had to face that hour,—to win that victory—as all the darkest hours must be faced, as all the hardest victories must be won—alone. It was not that He was above the need of sympathy,—no noble soul is;—and perhaps the noblest need it most. Though His friends did but sleep, while the traitor toiled, yet it helped Him in His hour of darkness to feel at least that they were near, and

that those were nearest who loved Him most.
"Stay here," He said to the little group, "while I
go yonder and pray." Leaving them to sleep, each
wrapped in his outer garment on the grass, He took
Peter and James and John, the chosen of the chosen, and went about a stone's throw off. But soon
even *their* presence was more than He could endure.
A grief beyond utterance, a struggle beyond endurance, a horror of great darkness, overmastered Him,
as with the sinking swoon of an anticipated death.
He must be yet more alone, and alone with God.
Reluctantly He tore Himself away from their sustaining tenderness, and amid the dark-brown trunks
of those gnarled trees withdrew from the moonlight
into the deeper shade, where solitude might be for
Him the audience-chamber of His Heavenly Father.
And there, till slumber overpowered them, His
three beloved Apostles were conscious how dreadful
was the paroxysm through which He passed. They
saw Him sometimes with head bowed upon His
knees, sometimes lying on his face in prostrate suffering upon the ground. And though amazement
and sore distress fell on them,—though the whole
place se med to be haunted by Presences of good
and evil struggling in mighty but silent contest for

the eternal victory,—yet, before they sank under the oppression of troubled slumber, they knew that they had been the dim witnesses of an unutterable agony, in which the drops of anguish which dropped from His brow in that deathful struggle looked to them like gouts of blood, and yet the burden of those broken murmurs in which He pleaded with His Heavenly Father had been ever this, "If it be possible,—yet not what I will, but what Thou wilt."

What is the meaning, my brethren, of this scene for us? What was the cause of this midnight hour? Do you think that it was the fear of death, and that *that* was sufficient to shake to its utmost centre the pure and innocent soul of the Son of Man? Could not even a child see how inconsistent such a fear would be with all that followed;—with that heroic fortitude which fifteen consecutive hours of sleepless agony could not disturb;—with that majestic silence which overawed even the hard Roman into respect and fear;—with that sovereign ascendency of soul which flung open the gate of Paradise to the repentant malefactor, and breathed its compassionate forgiveness on the apostate priest? Could He have been afraid of death, in whose name, and in whose strength, and for whose sake alone, trembling old men, and feeble maidens, and timid boys have faced it in its worst form without a shudder or a sigh ? My brethren, the dread of the mere act of dying is a cowardice so abject that the meanest passions of the mind can master it, and many a coarse criminal has advanced to meet his end with unflinching confidence and steady step. And Jesus knew, if any have ever known, that it is as natural to die as to be born;—that it is the great birthright of all who love God;—that it is God who giveth His beloved sleep. The sting of death—and its only sting —is sin; the victory of the grave—and its only victory—is corruption. And Jesus knew no sin, saw no corruption. No, that which stained His forehead with crimson drops was something far deadlier than death. Though sinless He was suffering for sin. The burden and the mystery of man's strange and revolting wickedness lay heavy on His soul; and with holy lips He was draining the bitter cup into which sin had infused its deadliest poison.*

---

* Is. liii. 4–6; Rom. iv. 25; 1 Cor. xv. 3. "Non mortem horruit simpliciter, quatenus transitus est e mundo...; peccata vero nostra, quorum onus illi erat impositum, sua ingenti mole eum premebant." Calvin ad Matt. xxvi. 37.

Could perfect innocence endure without a shudder all that is detestable in human ingratitude and human rage? should there be no recoil of horror in the bosom of perfect love to see His own,—for whom He came,—absorbed in one insane repulsion against infinite purity and tenderness and peace? It was a willing agony, but it *was* agony; it was endured for our sakes; the Son of God suffered that He might through suffering become perfect in infinite sympathy as a Saviour strong to save.

And on all the full mysterious meaning of that agony and bloody sweat it would be impossible now to dwell, but may we not for a short time dwell with profit—may not every one whose heart—being free from the fever of passion, and unfretted by the pettiness of pride—is calm and meek and reverent enough to listen to the messages of God, even be they spoken by the feeblest of human lips,—may we not all, I say, learn something from this fragment of that thrilling story, that—"being in an agony, He prayed." One or two lessons however slight—if any have ears to hear—let me draw from this.

For oh how much it may mean for us; not it may be to you as yet in the spring of life, though even you have had solemn warnings how death may stand unseen and silent even at the right hand of youth. But however bright the brightest of your lives may hitherto have been,—and may God your Heavenly Father make your boyhood very bright for all of you, that the memories of an innocent and happy dawn may refresh you in life's burning noonday and life's grey decline! yet for every one of you, I suppose, sooner or later the Gethsemane of life must come. It may be the Gethsemane of struggle, and poverty and care;—it may be the Gethsemane of long and weary sickness;—it may be the Gethsemane of farewells that wring the heart by the deathbeds of those we love;—it may be the Gethsemane of remorse, and of well-nigh despair, for sins that we will not—but which we say we cannot overcome. Well, my brethren, in that Gethsemane—aye, even in that Gethsemane of sin—no angel merely,—but Christ Himself who bore the burden of our sins,—will, if, we seek Him, come to comfort us. He will, if being in agony, we pray. He can be touched, He is touched, with the feeling of our infirmities. He too has trodden the winepress of agony alone; He too has lain face downwards in the night upon the ground; and the comfort which then came to Him He has bequeathed to us—even the comfort, the help, the peace, the recovery, the light, the hope, the faith, the sustaining arm, the healing anodyne of prayer. It is indeed a natural comfort—and one to which the Christian at least flies instinctively. When the waterfloods drown us, —when all God's waves and storms seem to be beating over our souls,—when " Calamity

> Comes like a deluge, and o'erfloods our crimes
> Till sin is hidden in sorrow—"

oh then, if we have not wholly quenched all spiritual life within us, what can we do but fling ourselves at the foot of those great altar stairs that slope through darkness up to God? Yes, being in an agony, we pray; and the talisman against every agony is there.

And herein lies the great mercy and love of God, that we may go to Him in our agony even if we have never gone before. Oh, if prayer were possible only for the always good and always true, possible only for those who have never forsaken or forgotten God, —if it were not possible for sinners and penitents and those who have gone astray,—then of how infinitely less significance would it be for sinful and fallen man! But our God is a God of Love, a God of mercy. He is very good to us. The soul may come bitter and disappointed, with nothing left to offer him but the dregs of a misspent life;—the soul may come, like that sad Prodigal, weary and broken, and shivering, and in rags; but if it only come—the merciful door is open still and while yet we are a great way off our Father will meet, and forgive, and comfort us. And then what a change is there in our lives! They are weak no longer; they are discontented no longer; they are the slaves of sin no longer. You have seen the heavens grey with dull and leaden-colored clouds, you have seen the earth chilly and comfortless under its drifts of unmelting snow: but let the sun shine, and then how rapidly does the sky resume its radiant blue, and the fields laugh with green grass and vernal flower! So will it be with even a withered and a wasted life when we return to God and suffer Him to send His bright beams of light upon our heart. I do not mean that the pain or misery under which we are suffering will necessarily be removed,—even for Christ it was not so; but peace will come and strength will come and resignation will come and hope will come,—and we shall feel able to bear anything which God shall send, and though He slay us we still shall seek Him, and even if the blackest cloud of anguish seem to shroud His face from us, even on that cloud shall the rainbow shine.

Yet do not think, my brethren, that, because God never rejects the prayer of sinner or sufferer, that therefore we may go on sinning, trusting to repent when we suffer. That would be a shameful abuse of God's mercy and tenderness; it would be a frame of mind which would need this solemn warning, that agony by no means always leads to prayer; that it may come when prayer is possible no longer to the long hardened and long prayerless soul. I know no hope so senseless, so utterly frustrated by all experience, as the hope of what is called a deathbed repentance. Those who are familiar with many deathbeds will tell you why. But prayer, my brethren, —God's blessed permission to us, to see Him and to know Him, and to trust in Him—*that* is granted us not for the hours of death or agony alone, but for all life, almost from the very cradle quite to the very grave. And it is a gift no less priceless for its alleviation of sorrow than for it intensification of all innocent joy. For him who would live a true life it is as necessary in prosperity as in adversity, —in peace as in trouble—in youth as in old age.

Here too Christ is our example. He lived, as we may live, in the light of His Father's face. It was not only as the Man of Sorrows, it was not only in the moonlit garden of His agony, or on the darkening hills of His incessant toil, that prayer had refreshed His soul; but often and often, every day during those long unknown years in the little Galilean village,—daily and from childhood upwards in sweet hours of peace, kneeling amid the mountain lilies or on the cottage floor. Those prayers are to the soul what the dew of God is to the flowers of the field; the burning wind of the day may pass over them, and the stems droop and the colors fade, but when the dew steals down at evening, they will revive. Why should not that gracious dew fall even now and always for all of us upon the fields of life? A life which has been from the first a life of prayer,—a life which has thus from its earliest days looked up consciously to its Father and its God,—will always be a happy life. Time may fleet, and youth may fade,—as fleet and fade they will; and there may be storm as well as sunshine in the earthly career; yet it will inevitably be a happy career, and with a happiness that cannot die. Yes, this is the lesson which I would that we all might learn from the thought of Christ in the garden of Gethsemane;— the lesson that Prayer may recall the sunshine even to the dark and the frozen heart; but that there is no long winter, there is no unbroken night, to that soul on which the Sun of Righteousness has risen with healing in His wings.

And that, my brethren, because true prayer is always heard. We read in the glorious old Greek poet of prayers which, before they reached the portals of heaven, were scattered by the winds; and indeed there are some prayers so deeply opposed to the will of God, so utterly alien to the true interests of men, that nothing could happen better for us than that God should refuse, nothing more terrible than that He should grant them in anger. So that if we pray for any earthly blessing we must pray for it solely "if it be God's will," "if it be for our highest good;" but, for all the best things we may pray without misgiving, without reservation, certain that if we ask God will grant them. Nay even in asking for them we may know that we have them,—for what we desire we ask, and what we ask we aim at, and what we aim at we shall attain. No man ever yet asked to be, as the days pass by, more and more noble, and sweet, and pure, and heavenly-minded,—no man ever yet prayed that the evil spirits of hatred, and pride, and passion, and worldliness, might be cast out of his soul,—without his petition being granted and granted to the letter. And with all other gifts God then gives us His own self besides,—He makes us know Him, and love Him, and live in Him. "Thou hast written well of me," said the Vision to the great teacher of Aquinum, "what reward dost thou desire?"—"Non aliam, nisi te Domine"—"no other than Thyself O Lord," was the meek and rapt reply. And when all our restless, fretful, discontented longings are reduced to this alone, the desire to see God's face;—when we have none in Heaven but Him, and none upon earth whom we desire in comparison of Him;— then we are indeed happy beyond the reach of any evil thing, for then we have but one absorbing wish, and that wish cannot be refused. Least of all can it be refused when it has pleased God to afflict us. "Ye now have sorrow," said Christ, "but I will see you again, and your heart shall rejoice, and your joy no man taketh from you." Yes, when God's children pass under the shadow of the Cross of Calvary, they know that through that shadow lies their passage to the Great White Throne. For them Gethsemane is as Paradise. God fills it with sacred presences; its solemn silence is broken by the music of tender promises; its awful darkness softened and brightened by the sunlight of heavenly faces, and the music of angel wings.

THE END.

www.ingramcontent.com/pod-product-compliance
Lightning Source LLC
Chambersburg PA
CBHW031747230426

43669CB00007B/527